MAKING A
MOTOR

MAKING A START IN
MOTORSPORT

SIMON ARRON

Published by

Sponsors of the
PSL Dellorto
750 Formula Challenge

In conjunction with the

First published in 1989

British Library Cataloguing in Publication Data
Arron, Simon
Making a start in motorsport.
1. Motor sports
I. Title
796.7

ISBN 1-85260-118-3

Patrick Stephens Limited is part of the Thorsons Publishing
Group, Wellingborough, Northamptonshire, NN8 2RQ, England

Printed in Great Britain by Woolnough Bookbinding Limited,
Irthlingborough, Northamptonshire

1   3   5   7   9   10   8   6   4   2

CONTENTS

FOREWORD

When I started racing back in 1964, the whole business of motorsport was a good deal simpler. If I had to start again tomorrow, I don't think I'd know where to begin, what with all the different formulae that are available to the complete beginner.

I think that a guide for aspiring competitors is a marvellous idea, not just to draw people into circuit racing, which has been so good to me over the years, but to attract people to the whole wide world of motorsport. There are too many people who don't realise how easy it might be to become involved, whether as a competitor or in some administrative capacity.

Hopefully that's all about to change.

My motor racing career has given me an awful lot of pleasure, and I would like to think that this guide will encourage a high percentage of its readers to participate in one of motorsport's many varied and colourful forms.

Your only regret will be that you hadn't thought of competing sooner!

Derek Bell
Double World Sports Car Champion
Five Times Winner of the Le Mans 24-hour race.

AUTHOR'S INTRODUCTION

The very fact that you are reading this *suggests* that motorsport means more to you than an occasional weekend television spectacle. Alternatively, you may be a curious newcomer, attracted by a fast-moving, colourful environment that is often sensationalized by the popular press. Either way, welcome to a world which stretches from the glamour of World Championship Grands Prix to muddy fields in the middle of nowhere, in which countless thousands derive an enormous amount of pleasure from their own particular arm of the sport.

It is an all-too-familiar tale that if one is to reach the sport's highest echelons money is as familiar a passport to success as natural ability. Bearing that in mind, how can the modest consumer even hope to penetrate the world which he or she knows only from the paying side of the spectator fence?

It may surprise you to know that it is not as difficult a task as it might at first appear. Have you ever considered joining your local motor club, for example? That won't transform you into a Hannu Mikkola or a Nigel Mansell in an instant, but it is a simple, inexpensive way of becoming *involved*, be it with organization and planning of events, navigating a friend in competitions, or simply watching, helping and learning.

Those whose childhood dreams had them winning the Monaco Grand Prix before a capacity crowd at an atrociously wet Monte Carlo circuit might nowadays be regretting that they do not have the thousands of pounds required to set themselves up in a novice Formula Ford championship. But have they considered other options? A trial day at a specialist racing or rally school, perhaps, where brief first hand experience is available for about £50? It isn't everybody's idea of motorsport, but as an introduction to pukka competition cars it offers unbeatable value.

For those spectators who simply aspire to take a more active role in the sport they love, there are numerous options. Marshalling, timekeeping, event organization ... there are several ways to increase your involvement, most of which will serve to benefit the sport whilst simultaneously adding to the satisfaction which you yourself can derive from it. Dip in to the following chapters with an open mind. None will turn you into a household name overnight, but that is not the intention.

Each chapter is designed to explain the basics of the many forms of motorsport readily available in the UK, some of which you may never previously have considered, some of which you may never even have known existed. An outline of what you will need in terms of cash and equipment to tackle each is given, together with advice on whom to contact if you wish to try your luck.

The purpose is simple. What follows should open your eyes to a few feasible options, convince you that there is motor-sporting life outside what you hear about in the media and above all encourage you to have a go.

Browse carefully, choose wisely, and you will find the sport rewarding, and in most cases far more readily available than you might otherwise have imagined.

Happy driving!

Simon Arron

1
CIRCUIT RACING

Obviously the first thing to do is to find money, and that's not easy. Presuming you have sufficient funds, karting is the place to start — the younger, the better. I really believe that anybody who has both pace and good technical ability in a Class One kart can be quick in a Formula One car later on!

When I started, driving in Formula Ford in England was good because it gave me the chance to do a lot of races, and to gain much experience. I think that it is particularly important to get used to the circuits you will need to know in the future. For that reason, I think that the new Vauxhall Lotus Challenge might be a sensible alternative for the karting graduate. For one thing, kartists are already used to slick tyres, so they would just need to learn about wings, and there are good opportunities to race in Europe, and therefore to learn circuits you'll find later in F3000 or F1.

The most important thing, though, is to race, and to gain experience, no matter what you're driving. If you aren't already based in Britain, I would say that any aspiring driver ought to come here because it still offers the best racing education in the world.

Roberto Moreno, Formula Ford Festival winner, race winner at Formula 3, Formula Atlantic, Formula 2 and 1988 FIA Formula 3000 champion. Now a fully-fledged F1 Grand Prix driver.

As even the most casual observer knows, Formula 1 Grand Prix racing is regarded the world over as the very pinnacle of motor sport. America has its own ideas about the cream of single-seater racing, which has spawned the potent Indycars (capable of lapping Indianapolis, from which they take their name, at over 215 mph (358 km/h)), but as far as international recognition is concerned, it is Formula 1 which matters; and that, after all, is the category which counts towards the official World Championship.

Whilst most awestruck schoolboys would gladly swap their satchel for the kitbag of a Prost or a Mansell, Grand Prix winners are not created overnight. It is a considerable challenge to extract the maximum from a 200 mph plus projectile, and even the superb handling characteristics of these cars were hard-pushed to cope with up to 1,000 bhp in mid-1980s turbo-charged qualifying trim ...

The path to motorsport's ultimate goal is a long one, frequently paved with heartache. Away from the commercial atmosphere which pervades modern Grand Prix racing, sponsors are an all-too-scarce commodity. Worse still, they are an absolute must if you want to progress.

Consider then that you are just about to start your racing career. In the mid–1980s, a full season of national Formula

Every young racer's dream? Alain Prost is the most successful Grand Prix driver of all time, but the road to Formula 1 is long, hard and can be painful.

Jaguar's successes in the World Sports-Prototype Championship have aroused plenty of media coverage. Like Formula 1, Group C is an arena for the world's very best drivers.

Ford at junior level might cost £40,000, if you were to mount a serious challenge. Without a bottomless wallet, you're clearly stuck. If you are lucky enough to find a substantial sponsor, all well and good; however, it is only natural that a sponsor should be interested in good results, and how do you achieve those without having the wherewithal to go racing in the first place? Catch-22.

Clearly, for those without telephone number bank balances, there has to be a way of getting started. So consider: do you view race driving as a potential long-term career, or is it simply something that appeals as a hobby? Either way, splashing out several thousands of pounds on a car could be a wastefully expensive exercise if you then discover either that you simply don't have the ability, or that the sport really isn't all you expected it to be.

Back to basics. There are ways to sample the sport without creating an irreparable hole in your wallet. The simplest step is to cast around for your nearest racing drivers' school, of which there are several dotted about the country. Major circuits such as Silverstone (Northamptonshire) and Brands Hatch (Kent) run their own, whilst there are also schools in operation at Oulton Park (Cheshire), Donington Park (Leicestershire), Thruxton (Hampshire), Cadwell Park (Lincolnshire), Snetterton (Norfolk), Mallory Park (Leicestershire), Knockhill (Fife),

Kirkistown (Northern Ireland), Aintree (Merseyside), Castle Combe (Wiltshire) and Pembrey (Dyfed). (See appendix for full list of addresses.)

Clearly there is no shortage of training centres, and their range of options varies from a simple trial lesson (usually under £50) to an intensive racing course which in the space of a week will take you from a classroom introduction to a race against fellow pupils at a public race meeting — providing you have passed all the relevant stages, of course.

The latter option might seem fairly costly. After all, once your week of fun is over, you are left with little but memories and — doubtless — the craving to continue. It is, however, excellent value for money. Consider the costs of preparing and running racing cars for novice drivers, whose previous lack of experience inevitably leads to the occasional expensive mistake — a missed gear and subsequently over-revved engine, or perhaps a twisted chassis in more extreme cases. It is soon apparent that the intensive racing course is a cost-effective way of getting your first real taste of the sport, since if you don't like it, it will have been a lot cheaper than spending several thousands of pounds to learn as much. If you did, it is still a sound investment. What you have learned during the week will certainly prepare you for your future career, and endow you

Which way? Formula 3 is a popular category for aspiring Grand Prix stars, providing an opportunity to learn about slick tyres, wings and close racing. Sometimes too close...

Final rung on the ladder to Formula 1 is usually Formula 3000, which brings together the cream of racing talent from all around the globe.

with sufficient knowledge to eliminate the risk of expensive mistakes you might have made had you entered the sport without prior preparation.

In short, to invest in a racing school course is to spend wisely. You don't have to blow your life savings on one frenzied week of activity. It is perfectly possible to spread your lessons over a period of time, according to your personal cash flow.

Whether or not you opt to hone your skills at a racing school, there are several things you will need before you think about going racing. Personal safety equipment is obviously essential; an approved crash helmet, fireproof overalls, gloves boots and underwear … kitting yourself out properly is costly, but essential. On top of that, you will need a competition licence from the RAC Motor Sports Association, the sport's governing body in Britain. Application forms are available on request from the RACMCA, and once you have successfully passed a medical examination you are free to apply. There are certain medical conditions which may prevent you from getting a licence actually to race, but there is little that will prevent you from being able to take part in one form or another of

motorized competition. Full details appear on the licence application form.

The cost of your licence will depend upon its grade. To begin with, each race successfully completed will earn you a signature from the prevailing RACMSA steward. The more signatures you collect, the higher the grade to which you are entitled; and the higher grade your licence, the more it will cost ... Whilst applying for your licence, it is also required, where appropriate, that you should apply for an entrant's licence and possibly an advertising permit, in order that sponsors' names can be given full prominence.

Licence aside, other bits of useful paperwork come in the form of club membership cards. Which clubs you join will depend upon which championships you are planning to contest, but membership of either the British Racing and Sports Car Club (based at Brands Hatch) or the British Automobile Racing Club (based at Thruxton) is often a prerequisite. There are, however, scores of smaller, regional organizations, membership of which will entitle you to race at national status meetings. (Again, consult appendix for details).

With racewear, licence and club membership in hand, you are in essence ready to go; so what about a car? In Britain, amateurs and professionals are completely spoilt for choice, with in excess of 80 British racing championships catering for a multitude of different formulae.

WHICH FORMULA?

To commence with the aspiring professional, his or her choice will inevitably be either Formula First or Formula Ford. These single-seater categories provide a healthy, competitive arena in which to develop your talents. Formula First was spawned

Top left *In 1988, the Vauxhall/Opel Lotus Challenge was launched as an alternative stepping stone for young drivers, immediately attracting full and competitive fields.*

Middle left *Many a career has been launched by John Webb's Formula Ford initiative, started in 1967 and still going strong.*

Left *Rising costs in Formula Ford led to the creation of Formula First, designed as an accessible starting point for the man in the street.*

in 1986 as a stepping stone into Formula Ford, which had previously been regarded as an ideal starting point. The latter's costs had escalated considerably since its inception in 1967, and Formula First was brought in to bridge the gap between novice drivers and the best part of the £50,000 they would need to finance a full season's racing, testing, travelling costs, petrol, race entries, accident damage and so on.

By way of consolation, success in Formula Ford can be rewarding indeed. The pick of each year's talent is inevitably creamed off by the leading Formula Ford 2000, GM Lotus Challenge and Formula Three teams, from where — the thorny problem of finance pending — careers can blossom sufficiently to attract the attention of Grand Prix managers. Take the meteoric rise of Ayrton Senna as a prime example. Blessed with a works drive with the crack Van Diemen team, Senna dominated British Formula Ford in 1981, repeated the trick in FF2000 (1982) and Formula Three (1983), before being snapped up by Toleman for a full F1 season in 1984. By 1985, he was a Grand Prix winner. In 1988, he was World Champion. Such a rise to prominence is every aspiring driver's dream, and Senna is ample proof that it can happen. If you have the motivation and the talent, you can go far, and the advent of Formula First has made it financially more viable to succeed in what is now recognized as a breeding ground for new talent.

Naturally, you don't have to invest five-figure sums to go Formula Ford racing. There are many regional championships, aimed at keeping costs down for local competitors. Virtually every British circuit runs its own championship nowadays!

In such series, a second or third-hand chassis will often be an adequate tool, and it might even be several years old. It won't be competitive against the contemporary chassis of the works or fully-financed private teams, but for competitive racing at relatively low cost it will be entirely suitable. The classified advertisement sections of the weekly motor racing journals are frequently full of such machines, the value of which has been sharply reflated by the advent of specific championships for cars built before 1974, those from 1974–78 and also those with the antiquated outboard suspension layouts.

Cheaper still might be a season in Formula Vee. The Vee chassis are based largely around Volkswagen Beetle standard running gear, and replacement parts are cheap. How does a

Production saloon car racing is well-supported, and invariably close...

...sometimes a little bit too much so for comfort.

Above *In spite of its age, the Mini still makes regular appearances on the British national racing scene, and is catered for by numerous one-make championships.*

Below *One-make series are not the exclusive domain of humble saloons. There are opportunities aplenty for owners of more exotic machinery, all of whom invariably try their hardest.*

Based around mainly standard components from the ubiquitous VW Beetle, Formula Vee is one of the cheaper forms of single-seater competition, as witnessed by its healthy state in the UK.

serviceable gearbox for £25 sound? The regulations have remained sufficiently stable over the years, so that it is still possible to be competitive with a car the best part of 20 years old. Formula Vee does not attract those with an eye on Formula One, but it enjoys healthy support from a happy band of amateur racing enthusiasts who really do enjoy a cheap brand of motorsport. And don't be fooled by the formula's apparent lack of development over the years. Lap times are only a few seconds off a competitive Formula Ford time at most circuits, yet your season's racing might cost you a twentieth of the price of the latter! Look around, and you are sure to find something to suit both your personal aspirations and your budgetary requirements.

Amongst the faster single-seater options available are Monoposto, Formula Four and Toyota Formula Three, all of which make full use of full racing tyres and aerodynamic aids, yet retain cost efficiency through use of older chassis and reliable engines which are relatively easy to maintain. The more ambitious amateur might like to try his luck in a pukka Formula One car, which is perfectly eligible to race in Formula Libre. The latter allows any single-seater to compete, and

Right *There are many owners happy to air their prized historic racers, although mistakes — if they occur — can be costly.*

Middle right *New isn't necessary. There are numerous regional and national series for proprietors of older Formula Ford designs. The Crossle 25F first appeared in 1974, and is still competitive in both Formula E and the 1974–78 challenge.*

Bottom right *There are series for hybrid saloons in many states of tune. All are generally popular with spectators, who often find it easier to associate with 'tin-tops' than they do with single seaters.*

encourages an interesting mixture of powerful racing cars of varying vintages to race together in a competitive atmosphere. This is often a colourful spectacle, but a little bit of experience is advisable before you rush off to purchase any such machine. Organizing clubs such as the British Automobile Racing Club (BARC), British Racing & Sports Car Club (BRSCC), British Racing Drivers Club (BRDC) and 750 Motor Club can always supply details of their respective championships, so don't be afraid to enquire. The range of options is truly vast.

SPORTS AND SALOON CARS

There is of course no obligation to leap into a single-seater. Sports and saloon cars feature prominently at race meetings throughout the UK, and both feature in myriad championships which, again, can be tailored to suit the needs of the individual.

As a starting point, the road saloon championships have blossomed since their introduction in 1983. The rules are simple; cars must be road registered and taxed, and must be driven to and (where possible!) from circuits. So long as a car complies with the aforementioned, and meets RACMSA approval as far as safety standards are concerned, then you can simply drive to a circuit, unload your picnic basket, practice, race, reload and return home. A more straightforward concept is difficult to imagine, and naturally the idea appeals to many who race the same vehicles that serve as family transport for most of the year.

One stage on, production saloon racing is big business, where considerable manufacturer interest lends weight to the category's standing. Over 100 cars and drivers registered to contest the major national championship in 1987. Success here

Motorsport in the UK boasts many formulae unique to these shores. Clubmans is just such a category, providing amateur enthusiasts with performance almost on a par with F3 for a fraction of the cost.

can lead to a drive in the UK's premier saloon series, the RACMSA–administered British Touring Car Championship, the technical regulations for which are tightly controlled according to the instructions of the FISA, the sport's world governing body based in Paris. Whilst professional saloon car racers are something of a rarity, in Britain at least, success in the BTCC can lead to a place with a top team in the prestigious European Touring Car Championship.

As with single-seaters, logical progression through the ranks is possible. Whilst top-line saloon racing may not attract the same world-wide media attention as Formula 1, it is no easier an environment in which to learn your craft. It is always popular with crowds, who are able to relate more easily to something that resembles what they themselves might use on a daily basis, no matter how highly developed it may be under the surface.

For the adventurous, special saloon racing allows extra-ordinary modifications to be effected underneath what are — or were once upon a time — family saloon bodyshells. In the mid-'70s, vehicles such as 7 litre Skodas and 5 litre Vauxhall Firenzas were a familiar part of the racing scene. Whilst such eccentricity has faded since those halcyon days, the hybrid saloons are still a popular feature, as are the less highly developed (and therefore less costly) modified saloons. Such forms of racing are sub-divided into classes within the races, so whilst buzzing hordes of Minis may be swamped by more potent machinery, their drivers are still chasing outright championship titles.

One-make racing has boomed in Britain in recent years, for both saloons and sports cars, and provides perhaps the closest of all forms of relatively low-cost motorsport. If you want to learn a little about cunning preparation and smart racecraft, there can be few better places to be than in the midst of a pack of 30 Ford Fiestas, Renault 5s, Minis or Metros; when permitted modifications are few and far between, performance differential lies mainly in the driver. If you can succeed in this environment, you are doing extremely well.

The Alfa Romeo Owners' Club, Ferrari Owners' Club, Ford, Honda, Porsche Club Great Britain, BMW and Renault all run series to cater for their own aficionados and, expensive as one or two may sound, the races attract huge entries. Suffice to say that virtually any type of saloon car can be raced in any one of a huge number of championships, and the meagrest of budgets can be enough to get you started.

Sports racing cars are by no means as prolific as either single-

Starting point. Road saloons should have an MOT, tax and be driven on the road to — and hopefully from — race meetings.

seaters or saloons, but there are nevertheless interesting possibilities, notably in the 750 Motor Club's own 750 Formula, which thrives on home-built specials, fitted with Reliant 750 motors (850 cc Reliant engines are also now allowed). Providing your engineering ability stretches further than a set of Meccano, this represents another sensibly-priced entry into motorsport, one in which the challenge of technical innovation can match the actual thrill of competition.

More powerful alternatives can be found in Formula 1300, Sports 2000 and Clubmans; the latter's 1,700 cc A class cars provide performance on a par with Formula Three, at a fraction of the cost.

Owners of classic machinery, sports, saloons and single seaters from a bygone era of racing, are frequently encouraged to race in the many historic formulae, which cater for all manner of old-timers. Realistically, this is not for the impecunious beginner, as such cars are usually valuable and thus costly to acquire. If you were to buy a tatty example cheaply, however, it might make a suitable restoration project which you could later use to race.

Make no mistake: historic racers take their sport seriously and cars are normally driven as they were built to be — on the limit!

Top of the saloon tree is the European Touring Car Championship, principally the domain of professionals, and dominated by manufacturers such as BMW and Ford.

The unlikely concept of truck racing has gone from strength to strength, and attracts crowds second only to those at a Formula 1 Grand Prix.

At the opposite end of the evolutionary scale, truck racing is an up-and-coming form of the sport. Articulated cabs may lack the finesse of a purpose-built single seater, but their drivers require considerable ability to handle — and make the most of — the brute horsepower. Again, this isn't necessarily an ideal place for the total novice to start, but so keen is Brands Hatch to develop new talent for truck racing that it has implemented a series for pick-ups, designed to attract the aspiring truckie! Now there's food for thought ...

FIRST STEPS

By now, you may be thoroughly puzzled. Such is the proliferation of possibilities in British motor racing that the newcomer to the sport can be forgiven for his or her initial confusion. Remember a few salient facts. The sport doesn't just exist for the benefit of aspiring World Champions. There is a recognized path to the top which the ambitious may follow, but there are precious few spaces on a Grand Prix grid. To make life more difficult still, money occasionally speaks louder than talent. If you still aren't discouraged, then good luck to you. With the correct blend of ability and 100 per cent determination, you have as much chance as the next person.

For everybody, the sport can be readily available for a lot less money than you might think. Contacting the nearest local

Left *Accidents happen in all forms of motorsport, but stringent safety regulations ensure that drivers are well-protected. Steven Parker (41) had cause to be thankful for his roll-bar at Mallory Park's notorious hairpin.*

Middle left *Classic saloons are relatively cheap to run, and come in many shapes and sizes.*

Bottom left *No matter what you race, you should always budget for the unexpected...*

centre of one of the national motor clubs is a simple, initial step that will quickly lead to useful contacts and friendly assistance. British club racing has none of the frenzied hurly-burly all too often associated with the professional sport, and folk are usually willing to help.

Keep an eye on the motoring press, and attend as many race meetings as you possibly can. That will soon help you decide what type of racing you feel would suit you best. Once you have made your decision, it is a straightforward task to ascertain which clubs administer suitable championships. You are then just a 'phone call away from obtaining a full set of technical regulations and other relevant information. And from then on, who knows ...?

Once you've prepared and polished your newly-acquired car, ensure that you register for your championship in good time to ensure you will be eligible to race. During the course of your racing season, it is important to submit race entries well in advance. For one thing, late entries cost more; for another, in a well-supported championship late applications may not guarantee an entry. Again, the relevant organizing club will be in a position to guide you on deadlines.

Attention to detail doesn't stop there. On the race track, you will be required correctly to observe marshals' flag signals, and to drive safely at all times. Accidents will happen of course but have too many of them and the penalties can be harsh. If the RACMSA stewards don't run out of patience, you will probably run out of cash. Each new signature you collect on your licence is a step in the right direction; the sooner you collect enough signatures, the sooner you will be able to upgrade your licence. This in turn entitles you to contest more prestigious events, at home and abroad.

Neither be dissuaded by labyrinthine lists of rules and regulations, nor by the spectre of financial commitment. If you

The vagaries of the British weather mean that drivers have to be adaptable, even in mid-summer!

have the mind to do it, you can take up circuit racing almost as easily as you might play soccer in your local park.

For around £50 (a couple of tanks of petrol) you could be on your way down for a racing school trial tomorrow. Why not think about it?

WHAT YOU WILL NEED

RACMSA restricted racing licence (which may be upgraded to national and — subsequently — international status as you gain experience). Application forms are available on request from the RACMSA.

Medical certificate (physical disabilities, eyesight problems, epilepsy and diabetes are amongst the conditions which may make you ineligible for a medical certificate, and hence a racing licence).

Crash helmet. This must meet with an accepted safety standard (e.g. BS6658-85A, SNELL 1985 etc), and must be adorned with an RACMSA approval sticker, available from circuit scrutineers or direct from the RACMSA. Cracked or damaged helmets, or those beyond a certain age, will not be accepted. A visor or goggles complying with the BS4110Y safety standard must always be worn in an open vehicle.

Fireproof clothing. Socks, boots, gloves, underwear, balaclava and overalls are a costly but essential part of any racing driver's kit.

Membership of a recognized national or regional racing club (e.g. British Racing & Sports Car Club, British Automobile Racing Club, 750 Motor Club, Irish Motor Racing Club, Scottish Sporting Car Club).

USEFUL CLUB ADDRESSES

British Automobile Racing Club (BARC), Thruxton Circuit, Andover, Hampshire SP11 8PN; telephone 0264 772696.

British Racing & Sports Car Club (BRSCC), Brands Hatch Circuit, Fawkham Green, Nr Dartford, Kent DA3 8NG; telephone 0474 874445.

British Racing Drivers' Club, Silverstone Circuit, Silverstone, Nr Towcester, Northants NN12 8TN; telephone 0327 857271.

Cadwell Park Racing Club, Unit 2–3 Warwick Road, Fairfield Industrial Estate, Louth, Lincs; telephone 0507 84248.

The start of any event is always crucial. Races can be won or lost on the grid, and a clean getaway is vital.

500 Motor Racing Club of Ireland, 2B Mount Merrion Avenue, Belfast BT6 0FR; telephone 0232 702139/692863.

Oulton Park Racing Club, Oulton Park Circuit, Little Budworth, Nr Tarporley, Cheshire; telephone 082 921301.

The RAC Motor Sports Association Ltd (MSA), Motor Sports House, Riverside Park, Colnbrook, Slough SL3 0HG; telephone 0753 681736.

Scottish Motor Racing Club, PO Box 5, 25 Market Square, Duns, Berwickshire; telephone 0361 82370.

Scottish Sporting Car Club, 2 Southview, Dalmuir, Clydebank, Dumbartonshire G81 3LA; telephone 041 952 1338.

750 Motor Club, 16 Woodstock Road, Witney, Oxon OX8 6DT; telephone 0993 2285.

Snetterton Racing Club, c/o Snetterton Circuit, Attleborough, Nr Norwich, Norfolk NR16 2JU; telephone 095 387303.

BRITISH RACING CIRCUITS

Aintree, c/o Aintree Circuit Club, 1 Tilney Street, Orrell Park, Aintree, Liverpool L9 8DT; telephone 051 525 5060 (the circuit has no permanent administration buildings).

Brands Hatch, Fawkham Green, Nr Dartford, Kent DA3 8NG; telephone 0474 872331.

Cadwell Park, Cadwell Manor, Nr Louth, Lincolnshire; telephone 0507 84248.

Castle Combe, Nr Chippenham, Wiltshire; telephone 0249 782417.

Donington Park, Castle Donington, Nr Derby DE7 2RP; telephone 0332 810048.

Ingliston, c/o 25 Market Street, Duns, Berwickshire; telephone 0361 82370.

It took a long, long time for him to convince others of his potential, but Nigel Mansell eventually did it, and came close to winning the World Championship on two occasions for Williams, prior to signing for Ferrari.

Kirkistown, c/o 500 MRCI, 2B Mount Merrion Avenue, Belfast BT6 0FR; telephone 0232 692863/642327.

Knockhill, Dunfermline, Fife KY12 9TE; telephone 0383 723337.

Lydden Hill, c/o William Mark Holdings, 71 West Street, Sittingbourne, Kent; telephone 0795 72926/71978 (the circuit has no permanent administration buildings).

Mallory Park, Kirkby Mallory, Leicester; telephone 0455 42931.

Oulton Park, Little Budworth, Nr Tarporley, Cheshire; telephone 082 921 301.

Silverstone, Nr Towcester, Northants, NN12 9TB; telephone 0327 857271.

Snetterton, Nr Snetterton, Norwich, Norfolk NR16 2JU; telephone 095 387 303.

Thruxton, Nr Andover, Hampshire SP11 8PN; telephone 0264 772607/772696.

RACING DRIVERS' SCHOOLS

Aintree Racing Drivers' School, c/o Malcolm Barfoot, 7 Andrews Close, Tarvin, Chester CH3 8LN; telephone 0829 41176.

Brands Hatch Racing School, Brands Hatch Circuit, Fawkham Green, Nr Dartford, Kent DA3 8NG; telephone 0474 872367. (Brands Hatch RS also has associated schools at Cadwell Park 0507 602944, Oulton Park 082 921381 and Snetterton 0507 602944.)

Jim Russell Racing Drivers' School, c/o Donington Park, Castle Donington, Nr Derby DE7 2RP; telephone 0332 811430.

Silverstone Racing School, Silverstone Circuit, Nr Towcester, Northants NN12 8TN; telephone 0327 857271.

Ian Taylor's Racing School, Kiln Meadow, Oare, Hermitage, Nr Newbury, Berkshire; telephone 0635 200205. (Courses take place at Thruxton.)

Castle Combe Racing School, Westway, Castle Combe, Chippenham, Wiltshire; telephone 0249 782417.

Tom Brown's Racing School, Knockhill Racing Circuit, Dunfermline, Fife, KY12 9XX; telephone 0383 723337.

Peacock International Racing Drivers' School, Kirkistown, c/o Crossle Cars, 217 Old Holywood Road, Holywood, County Down, Northern Ireland; telephone 0232 63332.

2
RALLYING

The first thing for any aspiring rally driver is to get involved with his or her local, active motor club, because participation in any way at grass roots level will give an idea of what goes into the sport.

The best tactic is to work your way up from club events, perhaps co-driving for a couple of rallies as a taster. There's no point starting off in powerful cars. Begin in the 1300 class, where cars are cheaper and more reliable, to gain experience and learn about driving technique. You will be perfectly eligible to win class awards.

As an absolute base starting point, you could buy a reasonable car, something competitive in one of the lower classes, for around £1,500. If you choose your events carefully I would add around £1,500 annual running costs, although much of this depends upon your own ability to maintain and service the vehicle.

Jimmy McRae, five times British Open
Rally Champion.

Whether rightly or wrongly, motorsport enthusiasts are frequently sub-divided into two species; racing fans and rally fans. This is naïve, of course, in that it completely overlooks the existence of numerous other worthy forms of the sport. Nonetheless, rallying can justly claim to be the most popular branch of motorsport at grass roots level. At its World Championship zenith, rallying receives nothing like the media coverage of its circuit racing equivalent, Formula 1, and consequently it is too easily dismissed as a minority interest. But as far as the UK and many other European countries are concerned, nothing could be further from the truth.

So what exactly does a rally constitute? Unlike racing, you need two people inside the car, and you try and beat your rivals against the clock, rather than in direct combat. Like racing, it is a competition in which the fastest, most consistent driver/navigator combination will triumph.

The driver's role is just what you would expect, but the safe and rapid passage across terrain that may be marked with any number of natural hazards depends as much upon the navigator's map-reading ability as it does upon the driver's skill. It will be the navigator's job to understand a map and provide ample warning of approaching hazards; tight bends, deceptive brows, narrow bridges, deep fords — all a regular feature of rally routes — as well as keeping an eye on time schedules.

Assuming that you intend rallying in Britain, bear in mind that most events take place on private land, whether it be through forests, around a disused quarry or perhaps using the facilities at an established race circuit, hired out to a motor club for the day. Public roads are occasionally closed so that they may be used as a rally stage, but this does not happen in mainland Britain, although the Isle of Man, Ireland and Ulster permit it.

There are, however, road rallies, which come in various standards of competitiveness. These do use public roads, which remain open to anyone during the course of the event. For obvious reasons of safety, these events take place around quiet country lanes in the middle of the night, and routes have to be carefully planned with the co-operation of the local police and neighbourhood inhabitants.

As you might imagine, road rallying has often been subject to controversy, and stringent regulations operate to ensure that speed limits are observed and that events don't run into opposition from angry locals. That the system works is clear; there are over 300 road rallies organized each year, and misunderstandings are as few and far between as mishaps in what is recognized as being a safe form of competition (it is not perceived as a 'race', thus overalls and crash helmets are actually outlawed).

Road rallies are not purely about speed, but require a delicate blend of team-work, with the balance between navigational and driving skills being dependent on the category of the event. When a road rally is announced, the organizers declare which Ordnance Survey maps it will cover. The navigator will be given route instructions before the start, or during the event, in one of two coded forms which must then be interpreted on the relevant OS maps. Drivers start at one-minute intervals and have to negotiate the route as swiftly and accurately as possible within given time parameters.

As the rallies tend to be off the beaten track, the routes take

The Audi Quattro started the four-wheel-drive revolution in rallying, and has survived the era of the Group B supercars. It can still be seen competing, on both national and international events.

Prior to the advent of the Quattro, the Ford Escort (here in Hannu
Mikkola's hands) had been the dominant rallying force, from grass
roots through to the World Championship...

...and it still forms the backbone of many a club event, and winning
rallies even today.

in all manner of tricky little lanes, and — for a navigator in particular — it is a marvellous way to cut one's teeth in the sport. Indeed, many of Britain's top rallymen, both drivers and navigators, began their careers in this branch of the sport. Legislation has tamed what was once regarded in some quarters as a rather irresponsible activity, but road rallying remains an accessible means of competition for almost anybody with a car.

The occasionally rough country roads may demand the odd precaution (fitting a sump guard, for instance), and powerful spotlights assist safe progress at night. However, it is fair to assume that you would not have to do a great deal to your everyday mode of transport (within reason — your Jaguar or Bentley may not be entirely suitable!) in order to go road rallying. It might not be a passport to success, but it is a simple way in. Road rallying remains a hugely popular activity amongst local motor clubs, and is a relatively cheap source of fun.

Those beginners who seek to compete seriously would naturally be best investing in a vehicle specifically for the purpose; bear in mind, however, that it is not a sport for anything *too* esoteric.

CHOOSING A RALLY

While circuit racing presents the curious beginner with a whole range of formulae and options to consider, rallying presents a more straightforward choice. Road rallying or stage rallying? Take your pick. If you are worried that your 1,275 Mini does not have the straightline speed of all those fully-tuned 2 litre Escorts, fret not. You may be competing on the same stretch of land, and will be out of the running as far as overall results are concerned, but rallying utilizes a similar class structure to that used in most forms of saloon racing on the circuits. Thus, vehicles of similar capability compete amongst themselves for class distinction.

Stage rallies again require the road rallying blend of teamwork, but higher speeds will concentrate the minds of both driver and navigator alike. *All* rally cars must be road taxed and registered, but the wise will always trailer their machine to and from events. Cars may depart the startline at intervals which prevents their colliding with each other, but stages are

You don't need to rush off and buy the most expensive car you can find. Class awards are available on all events, even major internationals, and setting your sights low is a sensible way to get started.

inevitably lined with trees, ditches and rocks which can — and often do — halt the unwary.

At base level, single venue stage rallies are a popular starting point. Within the confines of a given area of private land (airfields, quarries and race circuits are amongst the most popular choices), organizers will lay on a number of special stages. At the end of the day, the driver and navigator with the fastest aggregate time will take home the spoils.

Such events are the bread and butter of the enthusiastic clubman. You don't need to take out a second mortgage to equip yourself with a car, although a fair amount of preparation will be required if you are to be competitive. From the organizational point of view, restricting a rally to just one location keeps costs down and makes the whole thing relatively simple to monitor. In addition, it is usually possible to provide a mixture of tarmac and loose surfaces, and thus offer a suitably stiff challenge to entrants.

It is special stage rallying, however, to which most novice rally drivers aspire — and in Britain that usually means mastering Forestry Commission land. Special stage events utilize a variety of different locations, linked by sections of the public highway. The latter do *not* form a part of the competitive route, and participants' behaviour within these areas is always observed.

Rallying being an all year round sport, drivers will come up against all manner of adverse conditions, and rallies are seldom spoiled by the weather. The odd stage might have to be cancelled, but the competitors will nonetheless at some time be called upon to negotiate icy, snow-covered forest tracks barely wider than the car in which they are travelling at speed.

From inside the car, it is a different story. Drivers and navigators must have total faith in each other's judgement; if the latter advises that a bend may be taken flat in top, snowstorm or otherwise, then so be it. There will always be odd errors of course; it isn't unknown for the winner of the Lombard RAC Rally — the jewel in Britain's crown and a round of the FIA World Championship — to have inverted his car at some stage during his winning run. That is all part and parcel of rallying's hazardous nature; no map in the world is

Part of rallying's appeal comes from the spectacle it provides. Foot hard down, rear wheels scrabbling for grip and with opposite lock applied, Russell Brookes's Sierra Cosworth entertains spectators.

The end of the Group B era heralded a new dawn for rallying. The best of the production-based Group A cars were not as fast as their predecessors, but were still spectacular. The first team to master the new regulations properly was Lancia.

much use if a fallen tree has partially blocked the road, and you happen to be first car on the scene ...

Even if all this sounds like a precarious and foolhardy pastime, its popularity amongst competitors is more than matched by spectator interest. The Lombard RAC Rally attracts a huge following, and many will pursue the world's top rally stars the length and breadth of the country during the course of the event, staying up all night, every night to view progress through cold, wet forests.

The wave of enthusiasm is easily explained; externally, rally cars resemble the vehicles to which most people are accustomed. To see them conducted at high speeds across treacherous surfaces is something to which the man in the street can at least partly relate; moreover, it is enormously spectacular. A driver's flair, his ability to tread the delicate line between keeping his sliding car on the prescribed route and flying off into the nearest tree is there for all to see. If a car should slide off into a ditch, you can be sure that — 99.9 per cent of the time — there will be a crowd of onlookers to help push it back on to the road. It is a sport which the public finds accessible, and, even in such a relatively small way as this, one in which it feels it can be a part.

One of rallying's most pleasant aspects is that the true amateur can still compete in direct competition with the

world's best teams and drivers in events such as the Lombard
RAC Rally. Getting an entry is not easy of course, and you
must have attained a certain level of experience and ability, but
the fact remains that clubmen can compete in the same event as
the world's best; not on the same terms, of course, but rallying
is still a sport in which merely taking part counts for a lot. It
was in the dim and very distant past that amateur racing drivers
could think about wheeling out their second-hand Formula 1
car for their national Grand Prix. You will begin to appreciate
just why rallying appeals to so many as a competitor sport. It is
one of the increasingly rare sports in which a cavalier spirit is
allowed to thrive.

As with most forms of motorsport, your RACMSA competition licence will be upgraded as you progress. For a local event
confined to members of just one motor club, membership of
the latter may be sufficient if you wish to enter. On a wider
scale, however, a restricted licence from the RACMSA will
give you greater scope since, given time, this may eventually be
upgraded to international status — and then you may think

*Strict regulation changes have altered the face of road rallying
drastically. In spite of its name, this branch of the sport presents a
number of peculiar hazards, such as fords. Understanding between
driver and navigator is paramount. Helmets, fireproof overalls and
intercom systems are nowadays banned.*

Inset *Ford's RS200 was purpose-built for Group B, and became redundant when FISA announced its rule changes. In its heyday, it was hard-pressed to keep up with Lancia and Peugeot in the World Championship, although the odd national success came its way.*

Everybody has to start somewhere. Events such as the Lada Challenge exist entirely for the benefit of the clubman, and provide good, clean motorsporting fun at low cost. There is no substitute for experience, and this is a good place to learn on the cheap.

about tackling such as the RAC. Further afield, European organizers frequently encourage British participation in their events, arranging favourable entry fees and travel rates for the ambitious clubman and experienced competitor alike.

As far as pursuing championship titles is concerned, one can be as ambitious as one's means allow. For the relatively impecunious, regional series are commonplace, but there are prestigious national championships designed specifically for the enthusiastic amateur. Beyond that, the major national titles pitch professional teams and drivers against a mixture of aspiring newcomers and local hopefuls, the latter of whom can sometimes use regional knowledge to upset the form book.

To get your foot in the door of this ever-popular sport, which remains as pleasantly down-to-earth as its higher echelons as it does at its roots, there is no substitute for joining your local motor club. By all means get out and about, spectate, appreciate and breathe in rallying's atmosphere, but above all locate your nearest club.

Even the World Rally Championship has two targets for which one can aim. Although unable to compete on equal terms with four-wheel-drive opponents, Kenneth Eriksson's Golf successfully contested the two-wheel-drive class.

Snow business. On an event such as the Swedish Rally, four-wheel-drive is naturally an advantage.

There is no such institution in the land which does not — either independently or in association with neighbours — become involved in organization of a rally at some stage during the year. It may simply be a case of supplying marshals for a local event, or it could be promotion of a respected national rally. It matters not; the crucial thing is being involved, and where rallying is concerned, regional motor clubs are always at the thick of the action. Furthermore, they are inevitably packed to capacity with like-minded individuals and are a consequent hotbed of helpful advice and information.

Those who seek to jump straight into the hot seat should not be too disheartened, incidentally. In recent years, the sport has taken a leaf out of racing's book and there are an increasing number of training schools dotted around the country, each geared to teach a driver the rudiments of loose surface car control. Needless to say, a course of lessons is money well spent; learning how to do it before you attempt to drive through the trees is a whole lot cheaper than ploughing into them ...

Ultimately, rallying cannot offer the glamour of the international motor racing circus, but as an accessible form of motorsport it has few rivals. Consult the appendix for your nearest club, and you will soon discover why.

Too fast? Group B cars such as the MG Metro 6R4 have been outlawed from international competition, but may still compete on home soil. Plenty do so, which spices up the contest.

WHAT YOU WILL NEED

RACMSA rally licence. Navigators who do not intend to drive at any stage during the year may alternatively acquire an RACMSA navigators' licence (clubman and temporary licences are also valid for both parties). A medical certificate will be needed for stage rallies, for which certain conditions (such as diabetes or epilepsy) may render you ineligible. Road rallying requires no medical certificate. Application forms are available from the MSA.

Crash helmet. Normal RACMSA safety standards (e.g. BS6658-85A, SNELL 1985) apply, and helmet must be affixed with RAC approval sticker. Cracked or damaged helmets will be rejected at scrutineering. An intercom system should be fitted to enable easier driver/navigator understanding. Engine noise can otherwise disguise directions, which can lead to expensive accidents. Visors or goggles are optional, but recommended as protection against broken windscreens. NB: helmets must *not* be used on road rallies.

Protective clothing is not yet compulsory on all stage rallies,

Above *Rallying's structure is such that private entrants — such as Graham Middleton — can take on works teams directly, whilst also competing for class honours and — in this case — for Toyota's own bonus awards.*

Below *The Peugeot 205 T16 was one of the most successful Group B cars, until it was ruled out at the end of 1986 along with contemporaries such as the Lancia Delta S4. Nowadays, you might find the odd one in major rallycross events.*

but again is recommended — socks, boots, gloves, underwear, balaclava and overalls. Initial outlay is well worth it in the long run. NB: overalls must *not* be used on road rallies.

USEFUL CLUB ADDRESSES

Association of British International Rally Organisers, Auburn House, Dunmurry, Belfast; telephone 0232 621255.

British Association of Rally Drivers, 5 St Hildas Crescent, Sherburn, Malton, North Yorks YO17 8PJ; telephone 0944 70175.

British Trial and Rally Driving Association, Litfield House, 15 Cabstand, Portishead, Bristol; telephone 0272 84997.

Historic Rally Car Register, Droys Court, Witcombe, Gloucester GL3 4TN; telephone 0452 864341.

International Rally Drivers' Club, 23 De Verdon Avenue, Belton, Loughborough, Leics; telephone 0530 222958.

RAC Motor Sports Association Ltd, Motor Sports House, Riverside Park, Colnbrook, Slough SL3 0HG; telephone 0753 681736.

Rally Marshals' National Register, 11 Osberton Place, Hunters Bar, Sheffield S11 8XL.

Almost all regional and specialist motor clubs organize rallies. For a full list of these, please consult appendix.

RALLY SCHOOLS

Apex Rally School, Pembrey, c/o 35 St Non Avenue, Carmarthen; 0267 235155.

Bill Gwynne Rally School, Unit 17, Thorpe Place, Over Thorpe Industrial Estate, Banbury, Oxon; telephone 0295 51201.

Rally School Ltd, The Studio, Silverstone, Nr Towcester, Northants; telephone 0327 857413.

RSD Rally School, 1 Orchard Rise, Olveston, Bristol; telephone 0454 613394.

Welsh Forest Rally School, Cambrian House, Carno, Caersws, Powys SY17 5LV; telephone 0551 4201.

3
RALLYCROSS/ AUTOCROSS/ AUTOGRASS

The first thing to do is to go and watch a couple of rallycross meetings. Wander around and have a chat. It's a nice atmosphere, and if you ask a question people will always take time to answer.

The most obvious starting point for a rallycross newcomer would be Formula C, for cars up to 1600 cc with a maximum of two valves per cylinder, which gives you an enormous choice of cars, Escorts, Minis, Fiestas and Novas etc. Try to buy a complete second-hand machine. Keep an eye open for a competitive car that's available or, if you must build one yourself, choose a current shape. Something that looks the part will more usually impress a sponsor.

Keep things simple in your first season. Once you start tuning your engine, things start to break. There's no point trying to go too fast straight off; far better to be reliable, and learn about some of the driving techniques involved.

You should pick up a decent starting car for between £1,500–2,000, and running costs can be as little as £100 per meeting if you are sensible, and don't mind sleeping in a tent! A new set of tyres will cost about £280, so it's worthwhile buying part-worn rubber second-hand too.

John Welch, Motaquip British Rallycross
Grand Prix winner.

In motorsport, conversations about technological progress are seldom far away. No matter to what extent the international spotlight may focus much of this banter on Grands Prix, there are few — if any — forms of the sport which have matched the heady ascent of rallycross.

Rallycross was originally devised for television, as an attempt to bring together the most spectacular elements of circuit racing and rallying. Unlike rallying, cars would start four at a time, and the circuit would present a mixture of tarmac and loose surfaces. Drivers would still be racing against the clock, however, with those recording the fastest times during the brief qualifying heats moving forward into the latter stages of competition. In order to record a fast time, the immediate object was to defeat your heat opposition, and intense racing ensued.

It was immediately a great success, and remained a popular TV feature for many years. Gradually, however, media interest waned, although the sport itself grew in strength, particularly in Europe.

Its development led, naturally enough, to spiralling costs as the ever-increasing status of the European Rallycross Championship inspired development of some highly specialized machines. What was once the humble domain of the VW Beetle, Escort or Mini gradually became a playground for turbocharged sophistication and — ultimately — the Group B supercars. At the end of 1986, following a number of accidents (some of which involved spectators), the FISA — motorsport's international governing body — banned Group B cars (such as the Lancia Delta S4, Ford's RS200 and the Peugeot 205 T16) from rallying, in order to bring down speeds and costs.

The problem was what to do with the terribly expensive cars which were now redundant. It didn't take long before somebody had the bright idea of introducing them to rallycross. The result was that the European Rallycross series became even more popular, attracting huge crowds wherever it went, and enormous media interest in mainland Europe.

In a relatively short time, rallycross has become accepted as one of the brightest and most colourful forms of motorsport. Heats of eight or 10 cars are nowadays the norm, and in a European final most if not all will accelerate to 60 mph (100 km/h) in just a few seconds.

This spectacular rise naturally came at a price. If you are

Above *The Audi Quattro was amongst the first generation of rallycross supercars, and took Olle Arnesson to the European Championship title.*

Below *John Welch's highly-specialized Gartrac Escort slices inside Ivan Moakes's less glamorous example at Lydden. In spite of four-wheel-drive and enormous horsepower, the Gartrac Ford met its match when redundant Group B rally cars entered rallycross.*

Above *Ordinary mortals. Minis and Metros are common rallycross tools, and provide an ideal starting car for the novice.*

Below *Although generally taking the form of a high-speed time trial, with cars running one at a time, rough terrain makes autocross spectacular to watch, as London policeman Tudor Davies demonstrates. The versatile Escort is a popular choice amongst autocross racers.*

thinking that this is no longer the accessible means of competition it once was for Joe Soap and his Hillman Imp, you are quite right — at least at international level. However, aspirant rallycrossers need not despair. As usual, one simply has to look further afield, to find that there are alternative, more realistic ways to stick a foot in the door.

So let's start on home soil. Britain's own national series is healthy, and the wide range of classes and formulae (engine capacity, turbochargers and 4WD are all taken into consideration) ensures that those armed with a Mini or a relatively basic Escort, for instance, can still compete amongst themselves for honours, even if they can't hope to rattle those armed with multi-thousand-pound exotics as far as overall victory is concerned.

Further down the scale, the beginner could consider one of several regional championships, but bear in mind that there will inevitably be some top-class machinery entered, even at this level. Rallycross meetings are endowed with quality and quantity, right across the board.

Logically, acquisition of a reasonably cheap, reliable vehicle is as good a way as any to make a start. Unlike racing and rallying, rallycross has no proliferation of driving schools (although a rally school course would most definitely help you polish up your technique on the rough), so your initiation could be a trial and error affair. Just bear in mind, however,

As with any form of motorsport, mistakes can be costly. Rallycross heats are usually only a couple of minutes long, and bodily contact isn't unknown in the intensity of competition.

Above *Although rallycross has become the domain of the supercar in Europe, there has always been scope for innovation. Ole Wahlund's Beetle is turbocharged...*

Below *It may never have enjoyed success in other forms of motorsport, but the Fiesta has proved to be a superb rallycross machine. Competitive examples can be picked up relatively cheaply, and are a sensible means of introduction to the sport.*

Autograss involves direct competition against other cars, and is one of the cheapest forms of motorsport available.

that rushing out to buy the most expensive car available could be a short cut to an expensive pool of tears. Rallycross is close, and body contact is an accepted hazard; learn to walk before you try and run. You don't need four-wheel drive, twin turbos and 600 bhp to have some fun ...

If rallycross appeals, but looks too costly no matter how humbly you start, there are several related or similar alternatives which you might like to consider.

Minicross, for example, is hugely popular, and rightly so. The formula sometimes has meetings in its own right, and often supports major rallycross meetings. As the name suggests, it caters exclusively for Minis. The 850 cc engines are in a negligible state of tune, which provides good, close racing at genuinely low cost (as always, relatively speaking). The tight regulations bring driver ability to the fore, and with in the region of 30 cars starting each race, it is inevitably spectacular, and an ideal arena in which to develop one's racecraft. If things become a shade *too* close, competitors can take heart from the fact that spare parts for the ubiquitous Mini are as relatively inexpensive as they are plentiful.

If you feel you want a taste of the essence of rallycross, without making too serious a financial commitment, this is perhaps *the* ideal starting point. Standard Production

Above *What goes up, must come down. Mini spares are plentiful and cheap, which is probably just as well...*

Below *If it still goes, why worry? Tony Bibbs at Lydden Hill.*

*Ousted by the FISA from the World Rally Championship, the Lancia
Delta S4 found a home in the European Rallycross Championship,
courtesy of Matti Alamaki.*

Rallycross offers an alternative from a financial point of view,
but being exclusive to Lydden Hill, near Canterbury (regarded
as the home of the sport in Britain), it commands rather
localized interest.

Autocross used to be seen as rallycross's close cousin, but the
two branches of the sport are now relatively distant. In
essence, both are similar in that they involve competition
against the clock. In autocross, however, cars will often take
the start individually.

Autocross traditionally takes place on an all-loose surface,
fields being a popular location. The sport remains the domain
of the clubman, and has an enormous following throughout
the country. Indeed, the RACMSA endorses a major national
championship, and there are many regional competitions to
boot, with a healthy number of local motor clubs involved.

Part of the sport's beauty is that it welcomes all manner of
different vehicles within its class structure. Rally cars are a
popular weapon, as are standard road cars and home-built
specials. There is very little you can't use, and in some classes

Minicross provides fierce competition amongst hordes of evenly-matched cars.

the regulations do not require you to go as far as fitting a roll-cage, although those with any sense of self-preservation will do so as a matter of course.

For the aspiring competitor, it is a readily available and cost-effective branch of the sport, and one that is all too often overlooked. Glamorous? No. A practical way to enter motor-sport? Most definitely.

The same is certainly true of grass track racing, or autograss as it is known in some parts. On the face of it, autograss is a long way removed from rallycross, but for those who enjoy racing on the loose it is an excellent means of trying your luck *without* having to spend a fortune.

Like autocross, autograss frequently inhabits fields, but unlike the former, everybody starts at the same time, winners being decided in direct competition, rather than against the clock. In terms of pounds, the price of a fully-prepared grass racing machine should be somewhere in the low hundreds; with a little care (ie not running into the opposition, and keeping all four wheels on the ground), it is yet another ideal passport into some close, pleasurable competition.

We've turned full circle, from the costly world of inter-national rallycross to the more regionalized matter of autograss. Agreed, the two may look planets apart, but at the end of the day the latter provides loose surface competition,

Above *Rallycross sophistication. Quattros under attack from a Metro 6R4 and Ford RS200 at Brands Hatch.*

Below *People inevitably adopt a variety of lines through corners. A few of these are not recommended.*

which will help fine tune your car control and develop racing strategy. It is just one of several accessible starting points in this area of the sport, and who knows where any could lead once you've mastered them?

WHAT YOU WILL NEED

RACMSA speed licence (rally, clubman and temporary permits will also suffice for rallycross, minicross and autocross, racing, clubman and temporary permits for autograss). Not all autograss meetings are MSA-recognized, hence licences may not be required.

Crash helmet. This must meet with recognized safety standard (e.g. BS6658-85A, SNELL 1985), and must carry an RAC-MSA sticker of approval. Cracked or damaged helmets, or those beyond a certain age, will not be accepted. Visors or goggles are recommended, and must be worn in any vehicle with a perforated windscreen or not carrying a screen.

Protective clothing. Socks, boots, gloves, underwear, balaclava and overalls are well worth the initial investment.

USEFUL CLUB ADDRESSES

British Rallycross Drivers' Association, 21 Watermill Way, South Darenth, Kent DA4 9BB; telephone 0322 863605.

Minicross Drivers' Association, 48 Firfield Road, Thundersley, Benfleet, Essex; telephone 0268 778773.

National Autograss Sports Association, 21 Oaktree Avenue, Redditch, Worcs.

RAC Motor Sports Association Ltd, Motor Sports House, Riverside Park, Colnbrook, Slough SL3 0HG; telephone 0753 681736.

Many regional motor clubs organize autocross events. For a full list of these, please consult the appendix.

4

KARTING

There are many classes in karting, with a wide range of price brackets. Before parting with any money, go to a few meetings to see which class appeals, and ask around to see what you can afford. Once you've made up your mind, joining a kart club and acquiring a restricted licence will only cost a few pounds. If you want to get on in motor sport in general, there is no better background than karting for learning about racecraft and for developing your talent.

It would obviously be sensible for the beginner to start out with second-hand equipment. If you can find a helpful dealer attending the same meetings as you, try and form a liaison. That way you'll always have friendly assistance to hand. For the novice, that can be particularly important.

As a minimum guideline, you could probably scrape through a season for £700 in a non-gearbox kart, or around £1,500 in the 125 gearbox class. Comparatively speaking, even new equipment isn't too dear, ranging from around £700 for a new Cadet outfit to £5,000 for a Superkart.

Getting by at the former rates would depend upon your ability to maintain the equipment yourself, and wouldn't account for mechanical failures, but it should certainly be possible.

> *Martin Hines, 1983 World Champion, double*
> *European Champion, seven times*
> *British Champion.*

There will be few people who haven't encountered a kart at some stage during their life, even if the acquaintance was for but a few minutes in the pleasure park at some anonymous seaside resort. Do not, for a moment, be fooled into thinking that karts are mere toys, nor that this extremely competitive branch of the sport is a poor man's substitute for motor racing.

In its basest form, a kart chassis may be little different to the one-wheel drive, lawnmower-powered device you first tried when Uncle Stan took you to Southend-on-Sea for the day as an 11-year-old. From a mechanical viewpoint, rest assured that it is on a different planet.

At its highest level of technical development, karting has yielded the spectacular 250 cc Formula E Superkarts. With their enormous power-to-weight ratio, racing car-style aerodynamic bodywork, multi-speed gearboxes and tiny wheels, these microdot miracles will propel you along at somewhere in the region of 150 mph (250 km/h) when fully stretched. Given that your backside will be just an inch or so off the ground, that there is no true suspension to comfort you and that you may be just one in a field of 60 similarly-equipped hotheads, you will appreciate that it is seldom a sport for the faint-hearted.

In motor racing's overall structure, karting has a significant part to play. The proof? Look at the two dozen or so drivers taking the start in any World Championship Grand Prix, and ascertain how many of them cut their teeth in karting before transferring to cars. Mansell, Senna, Piquet ... They and a healthy proportion of their rivals started off in karting's humble playground. Indeed, an ever increasing number of capable young men making their name in racing share those origins. Cast an eye over the winners in Formula 3000, Formula 3 or Formula Ford; every year, the percentage of former kartists doing the winning is enormous.

Part of karting's great beauty is that it is available to virtually all ages. The RACMSA's introduction of the 100 Cadet class has opened the door for 8 to 12-year-olds to acquire a taste for motorized competition. Compared with a first season in motor racing, for example, your karting début comes cheap.

Throughout karting's various formulae, a maximum price regulation (covering chassis, engines and spare parts) ensures that finance doesn't get out of hand, but the aspiring Cadet's first requirement will inevitably be understanding, enthusiastic

Above *The advent of the Cadet class has opened the door to aspiring young racers as soon as they reach the age of eight!*

Below *With their streamlined body farings, Formula E Superkarts resemble scaled down racing cars. They are far from toys, however, reaching speeds of up to 150 mph (241 km/h) where circumstances allow.*

A pack of 125 karts streams into Silverstone's Copse Corner. As many as 60 might start each race.

and generous parents! Beyond the Cadet class, 100 Junior Britain karts cater for 11 to 16-year-olds; above that — irrespective of category — the minimum age for those racing on short circuits (less than 1.5 km) is 16, and on long circuits (over 1.5 km and permanent car racing facilities) 17. Theoretically, it is therefore possible to start car racing — Formula Ford for example — at the age of 17, with the benefit of several seasons' practical experience already behind you. You will begin to appreciate why kart racers tend to progress in racing circles.

That doesn't mean to say, of course, that you can't stick with karts throughout your competition career. There are many who do; karting may not have the glamour and commercial appeal of car racing, but on a national level at least it is likely to be financially viable for a greater number of people.

There is a wide spread of karting institutions throughout the British Isles. The RACMSA licenses over 40 circuits specifically for karts. Because of their size, karts don't require great expanses of space and consequently there are many temporary circuits, where barriers and safety facilities are erected and dismantled as required. Indeed, around 50 per cent of kart venues in the UK operate on just such a permit.

In order to keep entries at a healthy level, it isn't just costs which are strictly monitored. RACMSA regulations ensure that any clashing fixtures are sufficiently far apart geographically not to tread on each other's toes. In all respects, karting is governed in a practical, sensible fashion, hence its perennial popularity. It is thus only natural that there should be a logical path to follow if you aim to reach the pinnacle of the sport.

If you are a veteran of 16, you will have to bypass the Cadet and 100 Junior Britain classes, which leaves 100 Britain as the base starting point (although the more ambitious are perfectly

Eye on the future. This pair both enjoyed success in 100 cc karting before switching to circuit racing. Johnny Herbert (right) went on to win the Formula Ford Festival and British F3 Championship, establishing himself as one of the UK's top prospects and landing himself with a Benneton Formula 1 drive. Emily Newman tried Formula Ford as soon as she was 17, and was winning races within a couple of months.

entitled to try their hand at something more sophisticated). These karts feature direct chain-drive, and therefore rely on a straightforward two-pedal throttle and brake operation, although a clutch can be fitted if desired (the more powerful 125, 210 and 250 cc classes must be fitted with a variable ratio transmission).

The next step is 100 National, which allows wider engine choice and more liberal tuning. Competitors who race with success in 100 National may not be eligible to continue the following season, which encourages 100 Britain racers to graduate in the secure knowledge that they will have a sporting chance of success. Those who race with success in 100 National, and who wish to continue racing non-gearbox karts, can move on to 100 Super, which shares the same engine regulations as 100 National; eligibility is governed by driver ability.

The national gearbox classes cater for 125, 210 and 250 cc karts, which must have a minimum of three operative gears, and a maximum of seven, four and five respectively. There is a two-way division for the 125s, which race either in 125 National or 125 Open, the split governed by equipment specification rather than driver ability. At the top of the tree is the 250 International class, featuring the amazing Formula E machines to which karting's cream may eventually graduate.

That, in a nutshell, gives you Britain's karting menu, which in essence is similar to its worldwide counterparts (although

Karts as far as the eye can see. 250 Nationals get away at Cadwell.

the non-gearbox 135 cc Formula K and 125 cc Formula C gearbox classes are popular in Europe). Naturally, in order to progress you must upgrade your competition licence. As in car racing, you will start with a restricted licence; each time you complete a race satisfactorily, the clerk of the course will sign it to say as much. Once you have collected sufficient signatures (as specified by the RACMSA regulations), you are entitled to apply for a higher grade.

So how do you start? As with cars, there are training schools available although they are few in number, and in practical terms, these can save you a good deal of time and money later on. For the completely uninitiated, an introduction to one of the country's numerous kart clubs will be the most positive step; the sport's popularity means that there are a healthy number of such organizations.

During the course of a typical season (which runs from January through to December) the RACMSA will sanction something in the region of 300 meetings, from local club events at the likes of Clay Pigeon (in Dorset), right up to the British Kart Grand Prix around the expanses of Silverstone. Appealing though the latter undoubtedly is, stick your nose around the door at a more modest event, to begin with at least. That will give you an idea of the sport's roots.

It is a path which many tread; some in the hope that it will be the first step on a road to being motor racing's first 10-times world champion, others in the knowledge that — comparatively speaking — it is a cheap source of motorized fun.

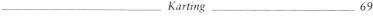

Left _For many years, Martin Hines has been Britain's 'Mr Karting', with a multitude of victories at home and abroad._

Middle left _Youngsters aren't spared the rigours of the British climate, and such tests stand them in good stead for the future._

Bottom left _At the top level, karting is truly multinational. Swede Lennart Bohlin is a former European champion._

The simple fact is that karts are cheaper to buy, maintain and run than cars, and a good deal easier to transport (a roof rack will usually be adequate!). As with car racing, however, it can be tailored to suit your own wallet and aspirations. It has an awful lot going for it, and it may take no more than a morning at a kart school to convince you of as much.

WHAT YOU WILL NEED

RACMSA restricted karting licence (which is eligible for upgrading as you gain in experience). Application forms available on request from the RACMSA.

Medical certificate (as with car racing, there are certain physical conditions which may render you ineligible).

Crash helmet. This must meet with the same RACMSA-approved safety standards that apply to car racing (e.g. BS6658-85A, SNELL 1985 etc), and must be adorned with an MSA eligibility sticker (available direct from the governing body, or from circuit scrutineers). Cracked or damaged helmets, or those beyond a certain age, will not be accepted. In karting, appropriate visor or goggles must always be worn.

Protective clothing. Overalls should be one-piece garments, in either leather or heavy duty PVC. Gloves (not mittens) must cover the whole hand and boots should cover and protect ankles.

Membership of an approved kart club (e.g. British KC, National Schools Kart Association, Wombwell Sporting Association KC, Central KC etc).

USEFUL CLUB ADDRESSES

Ace KC, 71 West Street, Sittingbourne, Kent ME10 1AN; telephone 0795 71978 (meetings at Lydden Hill).

Auto 66 Club, New Road, Nafferton, Driffield, North Humberside; telephone 0377 44727 (meetings at Carnaby).

Beccles & DKC, 12 Mill Road, Lowestoft, Sussex; telephone 0502 511829 (meetings at Ellough).

Birmingham Wheels KRC, 46 Standedge, Wilnecote, Tamworth, Staffs. B77 4LB; telephone 0827 895846.

Bolton KC, 26 Walnut Street, Bolton BL1 8LN, Lancashire; telephone 0204 28630.

British KC, Bank House, Summerhill, Chislehurst, Kent BR7 5RD; telephone 01 467 6533.

Bromsgrove KC, 28 Montreal Close, Lower Wick, Worcester WR2 4DZ; telephone 0905 42611 (meetings at RAF Little Rissington).

Cadwell C & KC, Armdale, Armtree Road, Langrick, Nr Boston, Lincs PE22 7AQ; telephone 0205 73361 (meetings at Cadwell Park).

Camberley KC, 43 Salcombe Road, Ashford, Middlesex; telephone 0233 57475.

Cambridge KC, 89 Chesterton Road, Cambridge.

Cardiff KC, Doghill Farm, St Nicholas, Nr Cardiff, South Glamorgan CF5 6SU; telephone 0222 593397 (meetings at Pembrey).

Central KC, 11 Sunny Grove, New Costessey, Norwich, Norfolk NR5 0EJ; telephone 0603 746218.

Chasewater KRC, 3 Morgan Road, Fazeley, Tamworth, Staffs B78 3LA; telephone 0827 57928 (meetings at Chasewater).

Cheshire KC, 107 West Vale, Little Neston, South Wirral L64 0SF; (meetings at Three Sisters).

Clay Pigeon KC, 257 Preston Road, Yeovil, Somerset; telephone 0935 71104 (meetings at Clay Pigeon).

Coleraine & DMC Karting Section, 41 Hartford Park, Ballygally, Coleraine, Northern Ireland; telephone 0265 56395 (meetings at Portrush, Aghadowey, Bushmills).

Cumbria KRC, South Farm, Celleron, Nr Penrith, Cumbria CA10 2LS; telephone 0768 65651 (meetings at Rowrah).

Dunkeswell KRC, 68C Deane Drive, Galmington, Taunton, Somerset TA1 5PR; telephone 0823 86365 (meetings at Dunkeswell Airfield).

Along with 125 and 250, 210 is the third of the gearbox classes. All divisions are sensibly governed by price restrictions, to prevent escalation of seasonal budgets.

500 MRCI Karting Section, 2B Mount Merrion Avenue, Belfast, Northern Ireland BT6 0FR; telephone 0232 491863 (meetings at Kirkistown, Newtownards).

Grampian KC, 106 High Street, Inverurie; telephone 0467 21705 (meetings at Boyndie).

Guernsey K & MC Karting Section, Lorelie, Rue du Clos, L'Islet, St Sampsons, Guernsey; telephone 0481 47847 (meetings at St Sampsons).

Hoddesdon KC, Kart Raceway, Rye House Stadium, Rye Road, Hoddesdon, Herts; telephone 0992 460895/461698 (meetings at Rye House).

Hunts KRC, Stone Court Cottage, West Land, Emberton, Bucks MK46 5DA: (meetings at Kimbolton).

Isle of Man KRA, Skibrick Ballabeg Road, Ballasalla, Isle of Man; telephone 0624 823884 (meetings at Jurby, Peel).

Jersey MC & CC Karting Section, Midway, Croix de Bois, Five Oaks, Jersey; (meetings at St Brelades).

Kingdom KC, 11 Tiree Crescent, Polymont, Falkirk FK2 0UX; telephone 0324 713950 (meetings at Crail).

Lincolnshire KRC, 43 College Road, Airedale, Castleford WR10 3EF; telephone 0977 556893 (meetings at Fulbeck).

Lion KC, 24 Morton Street, Middleport, Burslem, Stoke-on-Trent; telephone 0782 826069.

London KC, 53 Shearwater, New Barn, Longfield, Dartford, Kent, DA3 7NL; telephone 0474 72278 (meetings at Tilbury).

Merseyside KC, 20 Camdale Close, Stockbridge Village, Liverpool L28 3QD; telephone 051 480 1532.

National Schools Karting Assoc, 51 Stanley Road, Market Bosworth, Nuneaton, Warwickshire; telephone 0455 290538.

Norfolk & Suffolk KC, Olde Cottage, The Loke, Strumpshaw, Norwich, Norfolk; telephone 0603 715379 (meetings at Snetterton).

North of Scotland KC, 16 Drumrossie Avenue, Inverness IV2 3SJ; telephone 0463 221587 (meetings at Littleferry).

Northumbrian KC, 6 Valeside, Throckley, Newcastle upon Tyne NE15 9LA; telephone 091-267 7491 (meetings at Felton).

Plymouth KC, 60 Bridwell Road, Weston Mill, Plymouth PL5 1AB; (meetings at Riverside).

Plymouth KRC, 12 Shallowford Close, Edgebuckland, Plymouth, Devon PL6 5TN; telephone 0752 706923.

RAC Motor Sports Association Ltd, Motor Sports House, Riverside Park, Colnbrook, Slough SL3 0HG; telephone 0753 681736. (Organizes the British Kart GP, Silverstone.)

Shenington KRC, 1 Lisle Gardens, Bishops Tachbrook, Leamington Spa CV33 9QS; telephone 0926 883540 (meetings at Shenington).

Two Counties KC, Nightingales, Pilmoor BTM, Whiteshee, Holt, Nr Wimborne, Dorset.

Wombwell SYKC, 5 Redwood Glen, Chapeltown, Sheffield S30 4EA; telephone 0742 461278 (meetings at Wombwell).

KARTING SCHOOLS

Deavinsons, c/o Rye House Stadium, Rye Road, Hoddesdon, Herts; telephone 0992 460895/461698.

Playscape Racing, Buckmore Park, Kent; telephone 01 720 5226.

5

HILL CLIMBING AND SPRINTING

The best move is to get in touch with the Hill Climb and Sprint Association, to find out when and where meetings are taking place. Then go along to a few events to see which class takes your fancy. If you want to run a saloon or a single-seater, talk to somebody in a relevant class to see how they've gone about it.

Sprinting isn't a lesser sport, but is probably the best place for the beginner, simply because there is literally a class for absolutely everything. It is very accessible.

Assuming you already have a road car — and a basic Mini or Escort will be quite sufficient — you shouldn't need more than £100 to get started, taking into account club membership fee, competition licence and crash helmet. Thereafter, running costs are very much up to the individual, and whether or not he or she wants to buy new tyres and so on. It can be as cheap as you wish to make it.

Ray Rowan, 1981 British Sprint Champion and
leading hill climber.

'Age cannot wither her, nor custom stale her infinite variety.' Thus Shakespeare observed Cleopatra in his celebrated jottings about the latter and Mark Antony; had Britain's most illustrious playwright not been born the best part of 400 years too soon, he might well have ascribed this description to the average paddock at any modern-day hill climb or sprint. For variety is frequently the spice of motorsport, and never is this more true than in the case of these two closely-linked forms of competition, which provide complete novice and expert alike with an opportunity to take part in virtually any type of vehicle, be it an everyday shopping car or a purpose-built single-seater with 450 bhp plus Formula 1 engine.

But don't let the latter point dissuade you before you read further; the structure of hill climbs and sprints is such that competitors are divided into many classes where like vehicle races against like vehicle.

The essential difference between the two disciplines is quite straightforward. As its name suggests, hill climbing involves propelling your car up an ascending strip of tarmac, the idea being to climb faster than your class rivals. You are not racing directly against them, of course, but against the clock. Sprints follow the same principle, but tend to take place either on established racing circuits or on specially-marked courses at airfields or — occasionally — along promenades. That doesn't mean that a sprint is just a hill climb without a hill, however; a two-lap sprint at Brands Hatch will demand the same effort and precision as the battle to balance your car on the tricky camber at Shelsey Walsh. It is no surprise that many competitors dovetail a season of hill climbing and sprinting, taking part in as many of each as time and finances allow.

Top right *Ray Rowan began his competition career in sprints before moving on to tackle the hills. His March 842 started its life on the circuits as a Formula 2 car, before being converted to hill climb trim.*

Middle right *The start of any sprint or hill climb is crucial. Results are frequently decided on fractions of a second, making a clean getaway imperative. This is top sprinter Rodney Eyles at Bruntingthorpe.*

Right *There is a class for everything and anything, and the spirit of innovation is alive and well.*

No ordinary 'Moggie'! Nic Mann's Morris Minor is powered by a turbocharged MGB engine, and is hugely successful, not to mention popular with spectators.

Starting point. You don't need to go out and buy a purpose-built vehicle. Your shopping car is perfectly eligible for the standard road-going saloon class at any sprint...

...although sprinting also caters for such as Terry Clifford's Pilbeam.

The basic ingredients are therefore quite simple: during the day you can expect one or two practice runs, before the afternoon's competition, which, weather permitting, should allow you a couple of attempts to navigate the course faster than your class opposition. Any variation in the weather can, of course, dramatically alter your chances; if it starts to rain as you await your turn, tough luck. Conversely, it may be that the track is drying, and you will get a faster time than those who have preceded you. That's all part and parcel of the sport.

Unlike a race, where you may have 30 other cars around you to help you judge your pace and performance, you are all on your own in this branch of the sport. It is therefore imperative that you maintain 100 per cent concentration at all times, observing the correct driving line and judging braking points to a nicety. In a 10-lap race, you may have a chance to regain fractions of a second lost in momentary error. In hill climbing and sprinting, winners and losers are usually settled over an elapsed time of less than one minute. The slightest mistake is likely to cost you dearly, and a spin will rule you right out of the equation. Yes, you will get two bites of the cherry, but remember that a combination of speed and consistency will bring more success, and be a lot cheaper, than a kamikaze driving technique and numerous accidents. In the case of hill climbs, it is particularly worth noting that you will not have the luxury of a racing circuit's run-off area if you stray from the tarmac, and you may be stopped rather faster by a stout tree or solid earth bank than by your brake pedal!

Happily, the fact that you are in combat purely with the clock and the elements dictates that mishaps are far rarer in this branch of the sport than is the case in circuit racing.

Encouraged by this knowledge, what do you need to get started? A competition licence is required, that goes without saying, but you do not require a medical certificate, which opens the door to certain groups of people who may be barred through circumstance from circuit racing. Don an approved crash helmet, ensure that your chosen weapon is fitted with a suitable fire extinguisher and — providing the on-site scrutineers decree that it is fit to attempt the course — you are ready to go.

At the base level, you can quite literally enter your everyday family saloon. Class definition is quite liberal, e.g. road-going/production saloons, special saloons, modified sports

Clubmans chassis are popular in both hill climbs and sprints, their nimble nature and fine handling often letting them challenge more powerful machines for top honours.

cars, sports racing cars, single-seater racing cars and so forth. Each division will be further separated into classes, pertaining to engine capacity, so there should be a suitable hole on the entry list for your standard 1,300 cc hatchback. That is part of the sport's great appeal for the curious beginner who wishes to dip his toes in the water before making any firm financial commitment. By and large, it is also an arena in which the accent is firmly upon helping the enemy; assistance from fellow competitors is never far away, no matter in which class you might be involved.

Up above the basic road-going divisions, there is plenty of scope for innovation, and the carefree amateur spirit is admirably captured by numerous home-built specials for which hill climbs and sprints are exclusive terrain. Cars such as Nic Mann's immaculate Morris Minor, powered by a turbocharged MGB engine, have really captured the imagination over the years — and very successful they have been, too. It is an area where the technically capable can make their presence felt, and meticulously high standards of preparation prevail throughout all standard and modified classes.

At the very top of the tree is the over 1,600 cc racing car class. Whilst this attracts a certain number of second-hand chassis from the circuits (particularly in sprinting), it caters mainly on the hills for purpose-built single-seaters powered by a variety of highly-tuned, full race engines. This class represents the pinnacle of the sport, and a competitive performance at this level demands a supreme degree of driver ability, and — inevitably — a fair amount of personal wealth (or sponsorship).

It is the drivers in this category who will dominate the Top 10 Run Off at the end of a day's hill climbing. After the class runs, the 10 fastest drivers overall will go forward to take part in one final blast up the hill. In the RAC Hill Climb Championship, the UK's premier such series, it is the man who succeeds most often in the Top 10 Run Off who will take home the coveted championship crown at the end of the season. It is heady stuff, and very spectacular to watch.

The less ambitious/impecunious can of course continue to enjoy their sport in the sports car and saloon classes, continued success in which can bring both local and national recognition. Just as the RAC Hill Climb Championship is regarded as the highest target for those who like scrabbling up hills, so the RAC Sprint Championship is seen as the title to have by those who compete at venues as diverse as Curborough airfield, the

In this branch of the sport, venues are as diverse as the competing vehicles. The British Hill Climb Championship goes to the Channel Islands every year, for instance. This is Brian Moody's Ginetta at Jersey's Bouley Bay.

Left *Marc Cramer's father Chris has been one of Britain's top hill climb competitors for years. Marc himself preferred to start off with a Reliant Kitten, slightly modified, of course.*

Middle left *The class structure of sprinting helped Bob Forth to take the BARC national championship outright, with his Skoda.*

Bottom left *One to sort the men from the boys. Charles Wardle's Pilbeam is propelled up the hills by a five-litre V8.*

sea fronts at Blackpool or Brighton and part of the Isle of Man's notorious motorcycle TT course! Don't be misled to believe that racing against the clock is likely to be dull.

Naturally, there are numerous hill climb and sprint championships to cater for those without the time or money to go chasing the prestigious British titles, full details of which should be no further away than the national Hill Climb and Sprint Association (HSA), which caters for the needs of all competitors. Naturally, the RACMSA can furnish details of all recognized championships and can also provide a detailed calendar of events and respective organizing clubs; with in the region of 200 hill climbs and sprints taking place between February and October each year, don't be surprised if you feel spoilt for choice.

Generally speaking, hill climbs and sprints are strictly the domain of the amateur. On all its levels, the sport is conducted in a thoroughly professional manner, but the competitors themselves are usually happy to remain within this sphere. Some do branch out and try their hand at circuit racing, with success, it should be added; for most, however, it is strictly a hobby which hasn't been tarnished by the might of commerce which has nosed its way into some forms of motorized competition.

It is a happy-go-lucky atmosphere which encourages participation. Visit a chilly Brands Hatch sprint in February or a frosty Harewood hill climb in March, and not only will this give you a chance to scrutinize the enormous variety of competition machinery, and to see what takes your fancy, but also you will hardly fail to notice the predominance of smiling faces. As an initial venture into motorsport, it has much to recommend it, and the fact that few people choose to use it as a passport on to the international stage should not be a deterrent — far from it. At an advanced level, both hill climbs and sprints combine the need for both consummate ability at the wheel and a little engineering ingenuity; an introduction to this every-popular sport will present you with an ideal opportunity to develop your own talents in both areas.

Once into the swing of this competitive, yet friendly environment, why on earth should you want to try your hand at anything else?

WHAT YOU WILL NEED

RACMSA speed licence. Application form available from the RACMSA. No medical certificate required.

Crash helmet. This must meet with an accepted safety standard (e.g. BS6658-85A, SNELL 1985 etc), and must be adorned with an RAC approval sticker, available from circuit scrutineers or direct from the RACMSA. Cracked or damaged helmets, or those beyond a certain age, will not be accepted. A visor or goggles complying with the BS4110Y safety standard must always be worn in an open vehicle.

Fireproof clothing. Socks, boots, gloves, underwear, balaclava and overalls are a costly but essential part of a driver's kit.

USEFUL CLUB ADDRESSES

British Automobile Racing Club (South Western), c/o D. Wort, 16 Bond Street, Bitterne Park, Southampton SO2 4LP; telephone 0703 865711, x 297.

British Automobile Racing Club (Yorkshire), 41 Hoyle Court Drive, Baildon Shipley, West Yorkshire; telephone 0274 581333.

Bugatti Owners' Club, c/o G. Ward, Prescott Hill, Gotherington, Cheltenham, Gloucestershire GL2 4RD; telephone 0242 673136.

Hagley & District Light Car Club, 8 Compton Close, Solihull, West Midlands B91 1HR; telephone 021 744 7209.

Hill Climb & Sprint Association (HSA), 22 Silhall Road, Solihull, West Midlands B91 1JU; telephone 021 705 4229.

Midland Automobile Club, c/o M. Joseland, Woodbridge, Upper Sapey, Worcester WR6 6EX; telephone 0886 7411.

RAC Motor Sports Association Ltd, Motor Sports House, Riverside Park, Colnbrook, Slough SL3 0HG; telephone 0753 681736.

6
DRAG RACING

People in drag racing are nice and friendly, so get yourself involved with clubs and, better still if possible, with somebody already taking part. The more you become involved, the more contacts you make, and they can be invaluable.

You could quite literally start drag racing with an old banger and work your way up as you gain in experience. If you buy an old car, you can put a good, but not necessarily new, engine in it. It's just important to get the power-to-weight ratio right, of course. I started like that myself, and made gradual improvements and modifications as and when I could. I competed in just about every category before reaching the top class.

Nowadays, I reckon you spend as little as £2,000 to be competitive in the lowest street class, but if you do have a lump sum of money to spend, don't blow it all in one go. Save your funds for running and repairs later in the year. The best bet is to create your own little team, with each member contributing towards a kitty. That way you have something to fall back on.

Barry Sheavills, leading top fuel drag racer.

From a standing start, can you cover a quarter of a mile in a shade over five seconds? Indeed, would you want to when you know that those who can will reach a terminal velocity in the region of 270 mph (450 km/h)? Does all this sound like an activity for madmen?

Maybe, but there is no doubt that at its highest echelon drag racing is mightily spectacular. The aforementioned performance parameters are a regular feature of the American drag racing scene, where the leading competitors — professionals, by and large — are household names, thanks to widespread media coverage and copious amounts of sponsorship from major multinationals.

The picture isn't quite as rosy in Britain. Drag racing enthusiasts are as partisan as those in any sport, perhaps more so, but it remains something of a minority interest on these shores. Lack of facilities might partly be blamed; the total number of British drag racing strips can be counted on one hand.

So what exactly is a drag race? Simply put, it is a contest between two cars, held over a straight quarter-mile strip of tarmac. The first to reach the finishing line is the winner, and progresses into the next round. Competitions are always run on a knockout basis, until the original entry in each category is whittled down to just two finalists. But why should one want

Drag racing is a sport open to innovation. There are numerous ways of drawing attention to yourself.

Above *As in any form of motor sport, the start is crucial. This is particularly true of drag racing, in which there simply isn't time to recover from startline fumbles. Tyres are thus warmed up prior to the start, to obtain optimum heat and thus better adhesion.*

Below *While the sport remains on an amateur footing in the UK, America enjoys professional drag racing, with heavy financial input from manufacturers and sponsors. Drivers such as Kenny Bernstein are national sports stars.*

Brave lady. Shirley Muldowney successfully graduated to mainstream drag racing in the States, becoming a formidable competitor in the competitive top fuel dragster class.

to drag race anyway? Two cars duelling in separate lanes down a completely straight track may to an outsider perhaps sound a little dull. Outsiders be warned — it is anything but.

If you fancy having a go, forget the mind-blowing statistics at the start of this chapter, at least for now. Drag racing has numerous classes, and naturally enough there is a relatively inexpensive access point. In fact, you can get a useful introduction for no more than a few quid. Many low-key drag meetings operate what is known as a 'run-what-you-brung' class on pre-race practice days. For a minimal outlay of, say, a couple of pounds, you can have one or two blasts up and down the strip, using all the official timing gear and equipment.

This won't involve any form of direct competition, of course, but it enables you to acclimatize to official drag racing procedure. As you gain experience, your elapsed time should drop, and you can tune your reactions at the starting lights. This latter point is important. Known in the trade as the 'Christmas tree', the starting gantry is all-important. You go on green of course; leave before, and it's instant disqualification. The thing to remember is that the winner is the first to cross the finishing line, and is not always the *fastest*. Elapsed time is measured by a timing beam between two specific points

Dragsters don't have to be terribly expensive, and they come in all shapes and sizes...

...some of which are less familiar than others.

Steve Read blasts away from the lights. If you over-react and jump the start, you will instantly be disqualified.

one quarter of a mile apart. If you hesitate at the lights, you may run a faster time than your opponent over the fixed quarter mile, yet be beaten across the line and hence face elimination. Don't mock the 'run-what-you-brung' idea; it could save you much embarrassment later in your career.

You will need an RACMSA licence to compete on official race days, of course, and there are a number of places you may start. At base level, there are the street classes, in which competition vehicles must have a current MOT, to enable everyday road use. Cars may be trailered to and from meetings, but it is quite feasible to compete with the same vehicle in which you arrived. Equally, it is possible to spend a vast sum on tuning your street contender. Street classes are, however, subject to a performance index. For instance, a car in the Superstreet class must not be capable of covering the standing quarter mile in less than 10.9 seconds. That requires an *average* speed of almost 83 mph (138 km/h); when you take into consideration the standing start, you will soon appreciate that a high degree of acceleration is required. Not only must the car be up to it, but also the driver must make slick, and timely, gearshifts to maintain the best possible rate of progress.

In a nutshell, your season of street competition could cost you no more than the price of the relevant MSA licence, championship registration, entry fees, petrol bills and — vitally — a crash helmet. Overalls are recommended in street classes, but the only regulation is that arms must be covered. There are other saloon-based classes, such as Modified and Super Modified/Super Gas. These cater for more highly tuned saloon cars, and performance indices again usually apply.

Further up the scale, one finds 'funny cars' and rail dragsters. The former feature outlandish bodywork, based loosely around more familiar saloon shapes; the latter are sleek, low, pencil-slim creations, bearing no resemblance to any other type of racing car. These don't have to cost the earth; the mechanically-minded can save if motorized DIY is their forte. Engines are alcohol-fuelled, supercharged and fuel injected, and as a result the two different breeds may race against each other, as performance capabilities are similar. To aid prompt and efficient braking, such vehicles are equipped with parachutes!

It is a sport in which the impecunious may compete just as easily as those with more readily available cash. And if you

For all its fire and brimstone spectacle, drag racing remains one of the safest forms of motorsport. At the top level, drivers are protected by multi-layer fireproof suits.

wanted to make a career out of it? You'd have to look rather further afield than Britian ... Those with more modest ambitions can make it a rewarding hobby. Why not contact one of the national drag racing organizations to find out when and where you can participate in a 'run-what-you-brung'?

Beware of just one thing; the bug may bite. Once it does, don't expect it to loosen its grip.

WHAT YOU WILL NEED

RACMSA speed licence (race, clubman and temporary licences also eligible). Application forms available from the RACMSA. No medical certificate required.

Crash helmet. This must meet with an accepted standard (e.g. BS6658-85A, SNELL 1985 etc), as set out in RACMSA guidelines, and must also carry a valid RACMSA approval sticker, available from scrutineers or direct from Belgrave Square. Although not compulsory in *all* classes, visors and goggles are strongly recommended.

Fireproof clothing. Protection against fire is recommended in lower classes, compulsory in others. Where vehicles are fuelled by alcohol or nitro-methanol, drivers must wear multi-layer fireproof overalls, gloves, boots and facemasks. These tend to be costly, but are a vital and worthwhile investment.

USEFUL CLUB ADDRESSES

British Drag Racing Association, Bakersfield, 29 West Drive, Caldecote, Cambs CB3 7NY; telephone 0954 210028.

Midland Drag Racing Association, 27 Maple Road, Sutton Coldfield, West Midlands B72 1JP; telephone 021 355 2705.

National Drag Racing Association, 61 Chedworth Close, Church Hill, Redditch, Worcs B98 8QT; telephone 0527 63783.

Pennine Drag Racing Club, 2 Chapel Yard, Colton, Leeds LS15 9AH; telephone 0532 604442.

RAC Motor Sports Association, Motor Sports House, Riverside Park, Colnbrook, Slough SL3 0HG; telephone 0753 681736.

7
TRIALLING

Come and spectate to see if the events are to your taste and — if they are — join the BTRDA. That way you receive a quarterly magazine with a full calendar of forthcoming events. It's also worth taking out an RACMSA Clubman licence, which isn't expensive, and is a good way of getting hold of an RAC Blue Book, which gives access to motor clubs via phone numbers.

I recommend that anybody interested should get involved in some way as soon as possible. Offer your services as a marshal, or even as a passenger. There are normally vacancies, no matter what the event. Don't be frightened to ask questions. It's a friendly environment, and the more people you get to know, the more you will learn on the grapevine. It's a good source of free information! That way, you can often also learn about which cars are available.

It can be a very specialized field, so acquisition of a car might seem expensive, and you will need a minimum of £2,000–4,000 to get a reliable vehicle with which to start. On the other hand, depreciation is virtually nil, and if you don't subsequently find the sport to your liking, you can sell the equipment for whatever you paid for it. If you restrict yourself to within a 100 mile radius of your home, you should still be able to take part in a fair number of events for about £50 a time.

Julian Fack, multiple British Sporting
Trial Champion.

What do trouble, grief, an annoying person, a sheepdog competition and an effort to do something have in common? The answer, according to most dictionaries, is that all are definitions of 'trial'. Sheepdog department excepted, all sound rather arduous, agreed?

Fear not. As far as motorsport goes, trials give a tremendous amount of pleasure to an enormous number of people. Yes, they involve a certain amount of effort, and not a little finesse, but you are unlikely to encounter too much serious trouble or grief (or, indeed, any sheepdogs). There are numerous different types of trial, the most popular of which are production car trials, sporting trials, cross-country trials and classic trials. Getting confused? We'll begin with the first-mentioned, known in general as PCTs.

As the name suggests, competition is for production cars, split into classes according to a mixture of factors including length, engine size, engine/gearbox location and nature of transmission (ie front or rear-wheel-drive). Brand new machinery is *not* essential by any means; small saloon cars of 20 years old or more can still be competitive, and many successful vehicles have a good few years under their belt.

Competition is divided into a number of test sections, mainly on slippery ascents away from the public highway, treacherous fields being a popular venue. The idea is simply that a driver should — without stopping unless otherwise specified — negotiate the test as laid out between specified marker cones. If he is unable to coax his steed through to the finish (and within the prescribed route), he will drop a certain number of marks according to distance travelled. If you clean a section, ie pass through without incurring any penalties, no marks will be dropped. At the end of the day, those who drop fewest marks in each class will reap the spoils of victory. Where an overall winner has also to be decided, an index of performance will be established according to the top three finishing positions in each class, and marks lost will then be calculated as a percentage of this index, after which a winner will emerge.

Still confused? There's more. As if negotiating leafy, muddy banks was not sufficiently haphazard an activity in the first place, additional obstacles such as stop/start tests may be added to a section. Just as you are into your stride, with sufficient momentum to keep moving in the mud, you will be asked

Production Car Trialling excludes four-wheel-drive cars, and leaves competition to more humble vehicles...

...although you can be as adventurous as you fancy when choosing a suitable PCT contender.

Julian Fack, one of the country's top sporting triallists, reaches the summit. Observers stand at each marker point to ensure that competitors proceed in the prescribed manner.

to stop; fail to restart cleanly, and another helping of penalties will be on the way.

As they attract some the most humble vehicles to be found in any branch of motorsport, PCTs are easily within the means of most car owners. If you think you can come along with your four-wheel drive supercar and mop up all before you, forget it. Readily available 4WD vehicles may occasionally compete in a special class if specific event regulations allow, but may not compete for outright victory.

With an MSA licence, a few pounds for entry fees and several gallons of petrol, you can be in business. There are events on virtually every weekend throughout the year, and the myriad regional series are topped by a national series sanctioned by the RACMSA.

The story and the format are similar with sporting trials. The essential difference is the type of vehicle, in this case a purpose-built two-seater. Classes cater for vehicles up to

850 cc and those between 851–1,650 cc. It is delicacy and balance you need, not brute force. These curious, spindly vehicles are remarkably agile and equally rugged, which is just as well as tests will often involve circumnavigation of trees and mastery of all manner of narrow, almost vertical tracks.

Unlike PCTs, a driver must have a passenger on board, and the latter's role is essential when it comes to transfer of balance and weight distribution at tricky points. Passengers note: lean out too far or fall out and you will be docked penalty points! A competitor may also benefit from fiddle brakes, which control *independent* braking of each rear wheel.

Although acquisition of a custom-built vehicle, new or second-hand, will naturally involve a greater outlay than simply adjusting the tyre pressures of your everyday shopping

Cross-country trials are open to almost anything, irrespective of age. Dellow, Hillman Imp, MG Midget and Escort Van (!) line up during the popular Land's End event.

car for PCT usage, sporting trials nonetheless provide a low-cost (once initial expense is taken care of), friendly environment. What's more, two people per car participate, offering twice the opportunity to become involved.

Cross-country trials give owners of 4WD miscellany (Land Rovers, most popularly) to pit their skills against the elements, competitors judged on their ability to tackle wet, muddy obstacles (although some will also involve timed sections). It is a help if you and your passenger don't mind getting as wet and muddy as your machine ...

Last, but not least, there is the classic trial, which combines road sections with awkward stretches of both old public roads and private land sections similar to those on PCTs. Competitors are required to check in at various controls, and to remain within the bounds of a pre-arranged target time. Go too quickly, and you will be penalized. The spirit of challenge is the basis of competition; speed is of minor consequence.

The sporting trials car is a sophisticated piece of equipment, which is often just as well. Here, Ian Bell powers his way out of a rut.

Balance of power. Passengers must be prepared to put themselves around a little in order to assist the quest for traction. They have been known to fall out, which earns the team a penalty!

None of trialling's various guises can claim to be particularly high profile, and nor do they need to be. Simply, each has its accent firmly on sport. Every trial thrives on keen but friendly competition. If you're after a motorized hobby in pleasant company that requires a fair degree of skill and judgement, pitting man and machine against the elements without any untoward argy-bargy, then look no further.

WHAT WILL YOU NEED

RACMSA rally, clubman or temporary licence. Application forms available direct from the RACMSA. No medical certificate required.

Crash helmet. RACMSA-approved helmet (meeting stringent safety standards such as BS2495 or SNELL 1980) may be compulsory on certain cross-country events. Not required for sporting trials, classic trials or PCTs.

USEFUL CLUB ADDRESSES

Classic Trials DC, 18 Dane Close, Gwersyllt, Wrexham, Clwyd LL11 4SJ.

Essex Land Rover OC, Chalkmans Knoll, Bygrave Road, Ashwell, Nr Baldock, Herts SG7 5RH; telephone 0462 742418.

Midland Off Road Club, 101 Westley Road, Acocks Green, Birmingham B27 7UW; telephone 021 707 6557.

Northern Off Road Club, 2 Moor View, Bingley Road, Menston, Nr Ilkley, Yorks; telephone 0943 72453.

Northern Sporting Trials CC, Farlam Ghyll, Hallbankgate, Brampton, Cumbria CA8 2NH; telephone 0697 6233.

RAC Motor Sports Association Ltd, Motor Sports House, Riverside Park, Colnbrook, Slough SL3 0HG; telephone 0753 681736.

Association of Classic Trial Clubs, 3 Chipping Close, Symn Lane, Wotton under Edge, Gloucestershire GL12 7BB; telephone 0453 843497.

Scottish Land Rover OC, 10 Silverburgh Drive, Penicuik, Mid-Lothian EH26 9AQ; telephone 0968 76103.

Southern Counties Offroaders, 21 Broadhurst Avenue, Ensbury Park, Bournemouth, Dorset BH10 6JW; telephone 0202 514111.

Sporting Trials CC, 19 Tobernore Road, Magherafelt, Co. Londonderry BT45 5HB; telephone 0648 32327.

Most regional and specialist motor clubs organize trials of one sort or another. For a full list, please consult appendix.

8

AUTOTESTING

Basically the first step is to join a motor club, to put you in touch with what is going on.

To begin with, you should look for a fairly small family car, with good handbrake and brakes, and not too much power. That way it'll be easy to maintain and repair. Transmissions take quite a battering in this game.

All the same, it is a branch of the sport where you don't have to spend much money. Tyres must be road-legal, but can be well worn and therefore inexpensive. If you wanted to trailer your car to events, you could even start with something you picked up in a breaker's yard! That way, you need spend perhaps only £50 or £100 on a vehicle. Once you have a licence, you should bank on around £15–20 running costs per event. Depending on your car, you can usually find replacement transmissions for around £10 from a friendly scrapyard.

I know of several racing and rally drivers who have tried autotesting, and I would recommend that aspiring drivers try it before anything else. It's a marvellous way to learn car control before trying out the circuits or forests.

David Haigh, 1987 and 1988 RAC British Champion.

Who are the most skilful men in motorsport? Those whose steely nerve and millimetre perfect precision allows them to hurtle around the Grand Prix circuits of the world at speeds approaching 200 mph? Those who tear through forests, their cars sliding and twitching through the nearby maze of trees, ever teetering on the brink of disaster? Or could it be a hardy group of individuals who derive their motoring pleasure at a rather more leisurely pace in the likes of supermarket car parks and motorway service areas?

A preposterous suggestion? Not at all. The sport in question is autotesting, which is as much about perfect judgement and car control as it is about speed.

The scenario is simple enough. A course will usually be marked out by painted lines and those dreaded orange and white cones that drive everybody nuts on motorway journeys; such aggravating plastic pyramids serve a far better purpose in this environment. As you might expect, drivers must negotiate the course as swiftly as possible, without either straying outside the boundary lines or flattening the marker cones. Putting a wheel off course or striking a cone will simply earn you a stiff penalty, which will be added to the time recorded on the clock. It's a bit like the four faults a show-jumper will receive each time his horse demolishes a fence.

The sawn-off Mini is a popular, and most effective, autotesting weapon.

Noel Cochrane's MG Midget tackles a typical test. Competitors are required to move around the marker poles in a particular fashion, as quickly as possible...

...and occasionally backwards, too.

A different approach, and successful with it. David Haigh's Mayfly Special took him to the coveted RAC British Championship crown.

However, getting around the course is far from straightforward; it is also rather backwards and sideways. Confused? A beginner to autotests certainly would be. In order to follow the prescribed route correctly, competitors will need to carry out all manner of tricky manoeuvres. For instance, they may have to flick their car into 360° spins (probably both forwards and backwards during the course of the same test), reverse into tight spaces, double back on themselves and wriggle in and out of all manner of man-made obstacles.

It is rather like gymnastics on four wheels. Success is dependent on a delicate balance of finesse and technique. The handbrake is an essential tool for tight turns, and a driver must apply power carefully and at the right instant to maintain optimum momentum, without ever letting the car run wild and mow down the penalty-carrying markers.

The outcome of a day's competition will be based on aggregate times from a number of tests, which ensures that there is a reasonably full day's activity for all participants.

The most suitable vehicles? Small and nimble is naturally a good guideline, but — as always — there are classes to cater for all and sundry. Unlike most forms of the sport, however, class divisions depend more upon a vehicle's dimensions than its horsepower output.

Take the RACMSA's prestigious national autotest series, for instance. Saloons under 11 ft in length are divided into two classes, split at 1,100 cc, and there are additional classes for cars between 11–13 ft and over 13 ft. Sports cars are lumped together in one class as, too, are specials. Most popularly, specials are Mini-based, and usually differ from the original in having the bulk of the bodyshell removed, making for a lighter, more manoeuvrable vehicle and providing greatly improved rearward visibility.

You don't need to go that far to begin with, of course. The regulations actually allow for any vehicle, although common sense should tell you which are sensible propositions and which are not.

No branch of the sport can be guaranteed free of the odd mishap.

It isn't foolproof, of course. Vehicles used in competition get quite a hammering in transmission, braking and tyre departments, so be prepared to pick up the tab for spares during the course of the year, and to experience the occasional mechanical glitch.

Getting started? There are literally hundreds of motor clubs involved in autotest organization, many local, some based at universities or polytechnics. As usual, there is little substitute for contacting your nearest (see appendix) for details of events. Club membership will be sufficient to enable your participation in minor events, and the typical MSA licensing scheme applies otherwise, with upgrading to international status possible, experience permitting.

How popular is it? The simple answer is 'hugely so'. The MSA authorizes more autotests (between 700–800 would you believe?) in the course of a year than it does any other form of motorsport. The reasons are simple; it is a cheap, cheerful type of competition that puts a great onus on individual driver skill. Furthermore, it is open to just about anyone who has a car, and you don't necessarily have to have the fastest or the newest in order to succeed.

WHAT YOU WILL NEED

RACMSA speed licence (rally, clubman and temporary licences also eligible). Application forms available from the RACMSA. No medical certificate required.

USEFUL ADDRESSES

RAC Motor Sports Association, Motor Sports House, Riverside Park, Colnbrook, Slough SL3 0HG; telephone 0753 681736.

Autotest DC Northern Ireland, 11 Alandale, Bangor, Co Down, Northern Ireland BT19 2DF; telephone 0247 455471.

British Trial and Rally Driving Association, Litfield House, 15 Cabstand, Portishead, Bristol; telephone 0272 84997.

Almost all regional and specialist motor clubs organize autotest events. For a full list of these, please consult appendix.

9
OVAL RACING

In this game there's no substitute for experience, so I would recommend that anybody wanting to get into hot rod racing should start by competing in one of the cheaper formulae, like stock rods.

That will get you used to racing around a large roundabout in the company of 30 or 40 others, although you could always try being a taxi driver in London or Paris! Really, hot rod racing is no place for complete beginners, not when cars are worth in the region of £15,000 apiece. In addition, I wouldn't recommend banger racing to anybody wanting to move up to hot rods because it can get you too used to pushing and shoving. The best bet would definitely be one of the non-contact formulae.

You could pick up a basic stock rod for between £400–500, and I reckon you can normally budget on £30 per meeting running costs. That will start you off on the right lines.

George Polley, double World Hot Rod Champion.

It is a popular misconception that oval racing is motorsport's poor relation. In fact, the ovals envelop a whole range of different formulae, from the cheap and cheerful bangers to the technically advanced — and infinitely more expensive — hot rods.

Such circuits are usually housed in stadiums, the upkeep of which is often assisted by alternative activities, such as greyhound racing. More often than not, they are located in urban areas with a high catchment potential and — with all due respect — the setting can rarely match the glamour of Brands Hatch, let alone Monaco. As is so often the case, appearances can be deceptive. These humble abodes attract sizeable crowds to all the main meetings, drawing attendance figures that put those at some race circuits to shame.

The logic is straightforward. In length, a racing oval (its surface may be shale or tarmac) is usually around a quarter of a mile, give or take the odd yard. Spectators — for whom protection against the elements is nearly always available — can thus see the whole circuit and — if their wits are sharp —

The slippery ovals are a marvellous place to learn about car control. Young Paul Warwick did just that, in Mini Rods, before he was old enough to hold a driving licence. He has since progressed to the circuits, and Formula Three.

Stock cars are powerful, noisy and spectacular. The unusual triangular bar at the front is to assist with removal of the opposition...

perceive all that is happening around them. And wits do need to be sharp, for these tiny ovals may have up to 50 cars running around at any one time; the action is fast and furious, and seldom lacks in excitement.

Of course, certain oval racing formulae are designed to create thrills and spills. Take banger racing for instance. Motorsport could hardly come cheaper; a banger normally starts its life as an MOT failure in a scrap yard, and as such can be picked up for a few pounds. Preparation? It isn't just a question of stripping out the trim, fitting a secure safety harness and turning up at your local track. There is a technique, and those who learn the tricks of the trade will inevitably benefit.

Not that driving ability doesn't enter into it. This is very much a contact sport; if you can clatter a rival into the safety fence at 50 mph, all the better. If that sounds a frightening way to go racing, don't worry; it isn't. The safety record on the ovals is exemplary. Barging your opposition out of the way may be fun, but it can also inflict heavy wounds on your own vehicle. Naturally, there is a technique here, too, and the experienced banger racer knows just how to dispose of the enemy without harming his or her own chances ...

Oval tracks in the UK are controlled by a small number of racing organizations, each of which has its own rules. Some promoters do not make use of a roll cage mandatory in banger

Can you espy a straight body panel? Stock saloons take a lot of stick, but are suitably strengthened to cope with the rough stuff.

racing, others won't allow a banger to race at any more than one meeting (on the assumption that it will collect enough damage in one evening to render it unfit for further use). Casual as some of this may sound, it is actually the basis for a reasonable and workable system. Although this particular type of racing encourages endless accidents, from gentle spins into the retaining fence to destructive multiple cartwheels, impact speeds are normally low. Don't forget we're talking about a clapped-out vehicle rescued from the scrap heap for a brief career reprieve, not a 200 mph Grand Prix projectile.

The essential element? Fun. The best way to get involved? As always, go and take a look at your nearest stadium. Other formulae may come and go, but banger racing is an accepted part of oval motorsport throughout the country.

If you are wondering about banger racer mentality, think no further than the Destruction Derby which traditionally closes race meetings. Any vehicles which have survived the evening to that point are invited out once more; the last one running is declared the winner …

While you are taking a look, chances are you will notice some of the alternatives, which don't always involve trying to combine winning races with having accidents. At the opposite end of the scale to the humble banger are the hot rods. These are sophisticated, purpose-built racing machines which take a lot of time and effort to prepare for competition. Most start an evening's racing in gleaming condition, and most return home needing no more than a wash to restore them to that position.

As much as banger racing encourages hooliganism, hot rod racing condemns it. Touch another car and you'll soon be penalized; perhaps by one position, maybe a full lap — or you could be excluded from the racing altogether, depending upon the seriousness of the incident (accidental bumps may be forgiven, anything intentional is stamped upon in no uncertain terms).

As an illustration of driver ability, hot rod racing has few peers. Controlling a powerful, slick tyre-shod racing car at high speeds on a slippery surface in a confined space certainly sharpens one's concentration. Cars circulate just millimetres apart, and overtaking is far from simple. It is no surprise that some hot rod drivers turn into capable saloon racers. Although speeds may be higher on the circuits, hot rod racing has all the necessary ingredients to teach you about precise car control in heavy traffic, the like of which you will seldom see away from an oval.

The driver is not the only part of the equation, of course; several thousands of pounds may be spent developing a hot rod into a likely race winner, but no amount of technical wizardry

All forms of oval racing are noted for being close and competitive. Midgets are small, fast open-wheelers, with stacks more power than grip.

The cream. Hot rodding has its own World Championship at Ipswich every year. The sport's very best drivers have to qualify to take part, and they get quite a crowd to watch them.

can ever disguise a driver's shortcomings in such a competitive environment.

So, suppose you fancy a shot at hot rod racing? Won't you rather be biting off more than you can chew? Novices shouldn't be too concerned. There is a simple system applied to all forms of oval racing (although not always in banger racing, where it is often a case of first man out of the pit area takes pole position!) which takes into account driver ability. A competitor is graded according to his past results; newcomers will race with a white roof, experts with red, with those in-between graded as yellow and blue. White-graded drivers always start an event at the front of the grid, followed — at a slight distance — by yellows, another gap then blues, a further gap and then reds.

Those who have earned their spurs in the past must therefore fight tooth and nail to catch those whose inexperience gives them an initial advantage. It means that beginners spend their first few laps competing against rivals of similar ability and experience; when they are caught by the faster runners, they get a chance to try and hold their own, all of which gives them time to watch, learn and develop their skills.

As with most forms of the sport, there are ways of building

oneself up, in this case to the hot rod formula. Stock rods (known in some areas as Group A hot rods) provide a driver with ample opportunity to learn basic oval racing skills in a cheaper, less powerful environment (under Spedeworth rules, for example, cars run with standard 1,300 cc engines and road tyres). There is a very narrow band between good drivers and the indifferent, so racing is close and a bit of guile is required. Contact, once again, is frowned upon by the authorities; persistent misbehaviour will only lead to your downfall.

As previously mentioned, there are numerous formulae to be found in the world of ovals. Stock cars (superstox in some parts of the country), for example, are awkward-looking, angular single-seaters with a steering wheel that would look at home on your average double decker bus. In their ultimate form, these curious contraptions are propelled by 5 litre engines, which makes for spectacular high-speed racing. Here, contact is all part of the game and — all the while — you are meant to keep your foot firmly planted and control the car's direction with the considerable reserves of power activated by the throttle. Although still considered very much a minority sport, its supporters are as dedicated a bunch as you will find in any form of competition, frequently arriving bedecked in attributes to their own particular driver.

Midget racing does not have the national profile of stock cars or hot rods, but nevertheless provides a good deal of

Barry Lee was a giant amongst hot rod racers, one of the sport's most successful exponents of all time. He also proved his abilities in both rallying and racing.

Banger racing is fine for teaching you the rudiments of frantically close racing...

...or perhaps that should be the rudeness! Cheap and cheerful, some say it is not a good starting point for those aspiring to hot rods, simply because it can get you into too many bad habits.

pleasure for many. The single-seater midgets (which are as small as their name suggests) are less powerful than stock cars, but have crisper handling. Contact is out, the accent firmly on clean racing.

The latter is definitely not true of stock saloons, where stock car/banger tactics are encouraged from beefed up saloon cars, which by and large switch from scrap heap to competition career. The main difference between the stock saloon and the banger is that the former may be equipped with extras such as iron nudge bars to reduce the amount of self-inflicted damage in any impact. At the start of any stock saloon race, you will be lucky to see a single straight body panel in a field of 30 plus cars, but — like stock cars — they are considerably more durable than bangers ...

The variety of eligible categories varies from promoter to promoter. The simplest — and most logical — advice one can give is to contact your local stadium. It won't take long to establish just which categories are run at each venue, and one visit should be sufficient to give you an idea about the less than subtle differences between contact and non-contact branches of the sport.

Although hot rod racing is always close, deliberate contact is banned, and offenders are invariably severely punished.

After that? As usual, it is a question of personal preference, not to mention finance. Bear in mind though that there are oval racing categories to suit almost any budget. There are thousands who race regularly on Britain's ovals; if comparatively cheap sport is what you are after, you could do worse than to join the happy throng.

WHAT YOU WILL NEED

RACMSA speed licence. This will only be necessary if you are to race at an RACMSA licensed circuit. Most hot rod, stock car and banger races take place in stadiums operated by specialist promoters, where no MSA licence is required.

Crash helmet. No RACMSA approval required at non-licensed venues, but grasp of self-preservation and general common sense should guide you towards a quality helmet in good condition. Don't try and skimp on expense; a new, quality helmet can be acquired for less than £50.

Protective overalls. Fireproof clothing is recommended although not universally used. Common sense should again prevail.

USEFUL ADDRESSES

Incarace, 163 Bordesley Green Road, Birmingham B9 4TG; telephone 021 772 1060.

National Hot Rod Promoters Association, 163 Bordesley Green Road, Birmingham B9 4TG; telephone 021- 772 1060.

Promotasport Raceway International, Arena-Essex Sports Complex, A1306 Arterial Road, Purfleet, Essex; telephone 0708 867728.

RAC Motor Sports Association, Motor Sports House, Riverside Park, Colnbrook, Slough SL3 0HG; telephone 0753 681736.

Spedeworth International, Aldershot Stadium, Tongham, Nr Farnham, Surrey; telephone 0252 20182.

10
RACING OR RALLYING WITHOUT THE DRIVING

Throughout this book, we have looked at the maze of possibilities for the aspiring racer. Logically there should be something to suit every taste and every wallet. However, presuming that you do not have a sponsorship fairy, the cheapest possible forms of motorsport will still cost you several hundred pounds, and it can be horrendously costly for the foolhardy amateur.

Bearing this in mind, it is still likely that there will be some people who cannot afford to tackle their favourite branch of the sport from the driving seat. It could be that you did not fancy driving in the first place, but would still like to be involved in some way, shape or form. Relax in the knowledge that there will be a suitable hole you can plug in almost any form of motorsport.

MARSHALLING

Have you thought, for instance, of marshalling? Ever wondered where all those people in orange overalls spring from, week in, week out, come rain, hell or high water? Marshalling is not, repeat *not,* an easy way to get an unimpeded view of the action. It is often gruelling (British marshals have been known to suffer frost-bite during extreme periods of typically British racing weather), and can be dangerous (serious injuries are not unknown, nor — although rare — are fatalities).

What are the rewards for this curious and sometimes risky occupation? Huge financial gain? Well, you'll gain free admission to the circuit/rally stage or wherever else you might be officiating, but don't expect a single bean to top up your bank account. Satisfaction? Yes, you will certainly be able to take pride in what you do — if you do it responsibly. Being a marshal is not an opportunity for you to take photographs from an advantageous position, nor a convenient way for you to put one over Joe Public.

Many marshals attend a British Motor Racing Marshals Club official training day before ever setting foot trackside. It is a job which demands cool thinking and quick responses; imagine, you may have to extract an injured driver from an upturned car which is fiercely ablaze. An unlikely scenario, yes, but a possibility all the same. You will understand why marshals who react swiftly and correctly in certain situations deserve lengthy accolades.

A marshal's duties vary considerably. At a race circuit, for instance, there are course marshals (who must leap into action to clear away accident debris or restart stalled cars) and flag marshals, who must keep drivers informed via a recognized code of coloured flag signals. The latter job — which requires training — is another which demands sharp perception and clear thinking. Marshals will be allocated to posts, under the control of an observer (who must not only keep an eye on everything that happens on the circuit, but must also ensure that his cluster of marshals is performing to expectations). Some posts will be at

Marshals are the unsung heroes of motorsport. They are responsible for rescuing drivers from their mistakes, and have prevented serious injury and saved lives on many occasions. Note the medical officer rushing to assist at Oulton Park.

More trouble, this time at Thruxton. With several cars off the circuit, and one having vaulted the barriers, the marshals have a busy time ahead. The position of car 46 is proof enough that this voluntary job carries an element of risk.

notorious hot spots, corners at which cars may spin out of control or crash on a regular basis, others will be on harmless looking straights. Don't be fooled by appearances, as accidents can happen anywhere on a racing circuit (cars may not lose control in a straight line, but there's nothing to stop two or more colliding at speed), and should a vehicle try to self-combust, Murphy's law dictates that it will usually do so where you might least expect any dramas.

So let's get this straight. Being a marshal can lead to a busy weekend. On each day you must be ready for action well before practice actually starts (and that's always at a daft hour!); you will be standing, alert, on duty all day (it may be torrential rain throughout a meeting and you will be cruelly exposed to the elements), and may have a fair bit of running around to do (depending upon the whim of the drivers). And you won't get paid. In fact, your travelling costs (petrol bills, packed lunches etc) are likely to exceed the cost of the admission ticket you won't be paying for. So why bother?

That is strictly one for the psychologists. Logically, there are precious few reasons why one should want to become a marshal. Yet thankfully thousands do. Simply put, the sport could not exist without them. Typically, a marshal earns more complaints than plaudits; but such foolish criticism is best ignored.

So far, it seems there are few plus points. But as we've pointed out, motorsport could not exist without those who put

Chaos! Marshals, medical staff and the clerk of the course are on the scene at Brands Hatch. When a race has to be stopped, as it did here, the clean-up operation has to be swift to ensure minimum disruption to the day's programme.

in an enormous amount of effort simply through enthusiasm. The chances are that this will be reason enough for wanting to take the plunge. Socially, it can be quite rewarding and — perhaps above all — you will be *involved* in a significant way. On a sunny day, the course and flag marshals eke out a comparatively glamorous existence when you consider the timetable of a paddock marshal, pit marshal or assembly area marshal. Each dog will have its day though; one weekend you may be directing cars out on to the circuit, the next you could be working trackside, perhaps at the most spectacular corner.

As with any sub-division of the sport, there is a recognized path up which one may progress. Humble course marshals become, with experience, senior marshals, and eventually, perhaps, observers. At the top of the tree is the clerk of the course, whose job it is to see that the race circuit remains serviceable throughout the day, and to whom observers must report anything they feel deserving of a higher audience.

There are several clubs and organizations for those who

wish to devote their spare time to this curious pastime, which never ceases to increase in popularity despite some of its unusual demands on the human nervous system. Most of these organize training days during the course of the year; keep your eyes peeled on the specialist press, or simply pick up your 'phone and make a few enquiries. New marshals are always welcome and it is in the interests of the sport that there should never be any shortage of volunteers. You may not be appreciated by everybody, but you can be sure the drivers will be glad of your support.

SCRUTINEERING

Marshalling is not by any means the only way of spending free weekends knee-deep in racing cars for those who do not have a steering wheel to their name.

The technically-minded might like the idea of scrutineering, for instance. Before any car is cleared to take part in a race meeting, it must undergo a routine technical examination at the hands of one of a number of RACMSA-appointed scrutineers. If all is deemed in order, the driver receives a signed card which informs the paddock marshals that the car may be taken on to the circuit. However, if in the scrutineer's opinion a vehicle is inadequately prepared from a safety point of view or perhaps fails to comply with the regulations, it is the scrutineers' task to discover as much, and bar it from the meeting.

After each race, the scrutineers are frequently required to mount a secondary check on cars, to ensure that each raced in the same condition in which it was presented for morning examination.

It is a job that requires a good deal of attention to detail and a fair degree of intimate knowledge about race car engineering and the RACMSA's technical regulations. Consequently, it is a task for those with experience, although one is never too young to learn. Rather as drivers are licensed according to experience and ability, so scrutineers are graded. Those at the top of the tree may be given responsibility for international events, those in the lower branches might start out assisting at a single venue stage rally, or a Sunday afternoon club race meeting.

Scrutineers are scarcely the most widely-respected individuals at a race meeting, but their anonymity should not be mistaken for unimportance. For those sufficiently interested to undertake the job, it is rewarding and—most importantly — vital to the sport's safety.

TIMEKEEPING

When Murray Walker interrupts your peaceful observation of the Upper Volta Grand Prix to announce that Horace Screwloose has just broken the circuit record on lap 34, do you ever wonder how he has the information so readily to hand?

In the modern world of computerized everything, timing races has naturally been facilitated. Nonetheless, timekeepers remain an integral part of any race meeting, and it is a task which naturally demands the highest standards of competence and accuracy. Race timekeepers are required to chart with pinpoint accuracy the performance of every car and every lap it achieves. Their rallying counterparts are similarly pressed from stage to stage, and all equipment must be certificated to meet the RCAMSA's stringent standards.

Whether timing gear is automatic or manual, digital or analogue, its operators must likewise have been trained to use it to the same exacting degree. The fact that race and rally timing is seldom the root cause of controversy is testimony to the efficiency of those who click the stop-watches. Consequently, it means that timekeepers remain another rather anonymous body within the sport, yet they are no less worthy because of it. Without them, motor racing historians and archivists would have nothing to fall back on, qualifying sessions would be meaningless and rallies would quite simply be impossible.

If all you want from motorsport is to be usefully involved, timekeeping is a good place to start. How do you go about it? As usual, asking pertinent questions at a race meeting/rally (preferably during a lull in proceedings!) will furnish you with the basics, and the MSA can provide application forms for those who fancy trying their hand.

OTHER WAYS TO BE INVOLVED

Throughout the sport, there are areas in which people can make good use of their talents. Although this chapter takes racing as a prime example, there are marshals, scrutineers, timekeepers, etc, in all forms of motorsport, from rallying to autotesting.

More often than not, doctors and ambulance staff are thankfully required to do no more than stand by and watch. The unexpected can always happen, of course, and in the event of a serious accident the presence of the medical staff is as crucial as it is welcome.

Journalists, public relations men and women, noise test officials, tyre technicians, mechanics ... all may train to work a routine five-day week, yet there are places for all of them in motorsport.

It is a world full of diverse opportunities for people from all walks of life. The range of possibilities, and frequent ease of access to them, is something which relatively few appreciate.

Hopefully by now you will have seen a potential opening that suits your own taste and means; how you make use of that is up to you.

It remains simply to wish you every success in whichever branch of the sport you choose to pursue. Have fun!

USEFUL ADDRESSES

British Motor Racing Marshals Club, 2 Temple Close, Bletchley, Milton Keynes MK3 7RG: telephone 0908 78750.

RAC Motor Sports Association, Motor Sports House, Riverside Park, Colnbrook, Slough SL3 0HG; telephone 0753 681736.

Rally Marshals National Register, 11 Osberton Place, Hunters Bar, Sheffield S11 8XL.

Scottish Motorsport Marshals Club, 24 Barnshot Road, Edinburgh EH13 0DJ: telephone 031 441 2568.

11
SPONSORSHIP

No matter what you hope to achieve in motorsport, you won't get very far without a few pounds in your pocket. For those who intend to use a car they already own, and which is taxed, insured and ready to go, the sum will be considerably less than it would be for those with an eye on either Formula Ford or a major assault on a national rally championship.

It is difficult to impress a potential sponsor with your ability to promote them through motorsport when you never had the money to participate in the first place, so just how do you go about it? And, if you are sufficiently well-organized to draw in money for that invaluable first season of competition, how do you tackle potential backers 12 months later, when progression in the sport will inevitably mean greater cost?

As a starting point, there are some companies which specialize in finding sponsorship on an individual's behalf. They charge for their services, naturally, but if they produce results it is a wise investment. This is not a fool-proof method, but is worth considering if you have neither the time nor the resources to produce a proposal yourself. There are also companies which organize sponsorship seminars, and for a nominal fee, they will provide helpful advice based on their own experience of procuring financial support.

But let's get back to basics. Why on earth should any company, big or small, wish to part with hard-earned capital simply to see some young hopeful blow it on a racing car? Good question. The answer is that your benefactors will wish to see a return on the investment. It is no good simply turning up at the startline with your sponsors' name on the side. The car must look good, and so must you and your team. You should also be prepared to work hard meeting sponsors' guests, attending functions, endorsing sponsors' products and so on. This can be strenuous, more so than driving in fact, but

Left *The opportunity to sponsor a World Champion is an enticing proposition for any company. Camel's sponsorship of Lotus spreads to driver Nelson Piquet's helmet and overalls. Every available space is daubed in the corporate logo.*

Major multinational organizations do *sponsor young up-and-coming drivers in junior formulae, but those that receive such budgets are few and far between.*

if somebody is prepared to give you a chance to prove yourself, then surely the least you can do is to devote yourself fully to more routine activities on their behalf?

Motorsport *is* exciting, and glamorous with it. Any sponsors worth their salt will want to extract maximum publicity from their involvement, and it will be up to you, their driver, to fulfil that task. The more frequently you can get your name — and theirs — in the media, the better.

All well and good once you have found a sponsor, but that still leaves the thorny task of tempting a company to back you.

There is no guaranteed formula for wooing support, but there are a few simple guidelines to follow. Firstly, remember that a company is interested in *exposure* for its products, so your previous lack of experience/results may not weigh against you. The fact that you may have been south-east Hampshire's most successful rally driver for the past 18 months may *help,* but boasting of past and likely future achievements is *not* the way to introduce yourself.

One elementary prerequisite for the sponsor-hunter is smart presentation. When submitting a business proposal, make sure it is presented in businesslike fashion. Letters should be typewritten in accurate English, not scrawled in biro on a sheet from a ring-bound notepad. Don't expect a positive response to your first sales pitch. Don't even anticipate that you will fix a meeting with the managing director. Realistically, it could take hundreds, or even thousands, of letters to arouse the smallest whiff of interest from a handful of companies. There are lots of people bidding for sponsorship in all walks of life, not just from motorsport. You may have to sell them the sport before you sell yourself.

Have no illusions; it won't be easy. A sensible, businesslike approach will, however, at least give you a chance. If you pay for the assembly of a professional brochure, for instance, promoting not just yourself but the value of motorsport as an advertising medium, it might cost you a low four-figure sum, but if you are chasing a £50,000 sponsorship contract, it *could*

Spot the sponsor. For most club racers, the largest decals on their car will be race numbers.

Formula 1 teams know how to maximize advertising space, including that on the drivers. To have your name stitched on to the overalls of Prost, Senna or Boutsen costs plenty!

be money well spent. Certainly, those you approach will perceive that you are serious.

Targetting a potential sponsor is another matter for considerable thought. Anybody taking part in the East of Scotland rally championship would be a foolish optimist if he approached a firm doing business exclusively in Sussex. You have to weigh up the circumstances. If you are contesting any championship, national or regional, make sure that your local media knows about it. Establish contact with newspapers and radio stations. A publicity-seeking sponsor will be relying upon your own media awareness.

Is this beginning to sound like it may involve a lot of effort? Good, because it will.

Right *Smart presentation is essential, and draws attention to your sponsor. A sensible approach can net backing at national level, and provides ample marketing opportunities. When Mark Hales's Sierra won, Firestone was not slow to advertise the fact.*

Above *Like racing, top level rallying demands high levels of financial input, and that makes major sponsorship a necessity.*

Below *There are several ways of bringing your sponsor's name to the fore, but some are better than others...*

In Formula 1,
major sponsors issue
professionally produced
newsletters before each race.

There will always be those with access to sufficient funds to finance their participation in whatever branch of motorsport they choose. They are the lucky ones, and for every such case there will be dozens whose burning ambition is matched in stature only by the void in their bank balance! It is the latter group who will have to go in for the hard sell, tirelessly writing letters and knocking on doors, patiently explaining the value of advertising in motorsport and accepting negative responses with dignity intact and determination unbowed. Tough, but that's the way it is.

Bearing in mind the size of the task, it is *imperative* that you consider your every tactic most carefully before rushing in. Writing begging letters will get you nowhere. You must put together a bright, innovative and convincing promotional package. Such things take time, money and endless hours of detailed preparation, all of which will be justified many times over if and when you pull in your first major sponsor. Note use of the word 'if'. Even the most carefully formulated proposals are no passport to success, but they will maximize your chances of attracting support.

It may be that your sporting plans don't run to a complete season of national Formula Ford races. Maybe you have budgeted on £5,000 for a regional series in a second-hand car. Whilst your monetary requirements may be different, your approach must not. It is no easier to find £5,000 than it is to find £50,000 if you don't present a convincing set of reasons as to why anybody should want to dip into their funds to help you.

Finding sponsorship is a multi-million dollar business nowadays, and must be treated as such. That isn't to say that there's no place for the enthusiastic club competitor who is looking for a fraction of your average telephone number Grand Prix budget, but it does mean that a full, professional approach is required. Sit down and think about it. Calculate how you can turn your racing to the advantage of a sponsor, and how best to convince them of as much. In many ways it is a question of common sense.

Be sensible, be smart and above all be patient.

Good luck!

APPENDIX 1:
RACMSA ADDRESSES

The following is a list of the addresses of all clubs affiliated to the RACMSA Ltd. Details provided are correct at the time of writing, but may be subject to change. For latest information, please phone the RACMSA on 0753 681736.

B. Jones, ABERYSTWYTH DMC LTD, 21 Bryn Ystwyth, Penparcau, Aberystwyth, Dyfed SY23 1SS

D. Mackintosh, ABERDEEN & DMC LTD, 6 Nethermains Road, Muchalls, Stonehaven, Kincardineshire

D. Higgs, ABERGAVENNY AC, 2 Meadway, Abergavenny, Gwent NP7 6BW

Douglas R. Weir, ABERDEEN UNIVERSITY MC, 101 Jesmond Roadens, Bridge of Don, Aberdeen AB2 8NY

J.P. Dine, ACOC LTD, Stoke Lodge, Aldersey Road, Guildford, Surrey GU1 2ES

B. Harris, ACE KC, 71 West Street, Sittingbourne, Kent ME10 1AN

M.J.P. Ashcroft, AINTREE CIRCUIT CLUB, 1 Tilney Street, Orrell Park, Aintree, Liverpool L9 8DT

I. Morton, AIREDALE & PENNINE MCC, 42 Marshfield Street, Marshfield, Bradford BD5 9NB

M. Lindsay, ALFA ROMEO OC LTD, 97 High Street, Linton, Cambridge CB1 6JT

Miss P. Hulse, ALLARD OC, 1 Dalmeny Avenue, Tufnell Park, London N7 0LD

M. Surgenor, ALLOA & DMC, 42 Slamannan Road, Falkirk, Stirlingshire FK1 3BW

S. McCutcheon, ALL WHEEL DC, 41 Montem Road, New Malden, Surrey KT3 3QU

F. Imeson, ALNWICK & DMC, 15 Duke Street, Alnwick, Northumberland NE66 1QU

B.R. Chant, ALVIS OC, Milestones, Grove Lane, Stalbridge, Dorset DT10 2RF

Ms J. Elliot, ALWOODLEY MC, 9 Meadow Way, Alwoodley, Leeds LS17 7QY

R. Whitney, AMMAN & DMC, 8 Underwood Road, Cadoxton, Neath, Glamorgan SA10 8BU

Mr H.G. Llewellyn Evans, THE AMMANFORD MOTOR CLUB, 61 Greenfield Crescent, Llansamlet, Swansea, West Glam. SA7 9SL

A.J. Flanders, ANGLIAN ROC, 3 Mortimer Hill, Tring, Herts. HP23 5JT

Colin Hunt, ANGLIAN RALLY CLUB, 68 Raynham Road, Bury St Edmunds, Suffolk IP32 6ED

John Russell, APEX MOTOR CLUB (SCOTLAND), 9 St Brides Road, Newlands, Glasgow G43 2DU

Mr P. McCann, ARBROATH & DISTRICT MC, 63 East Kirkton Road, Arbroath, Angus DD11 4HR

Mr D. Phelps, ASHFORD KENT MC, 27 Crownfield Road, South Ashford, Kent TN23 2ED

J. West, ASSN OF CLASSIC TRIAL CLUBS, 3 Chipping Close, Symn Lane, Wotton Under Edge, Gloucestershire GL12 7BB

G.R. Day, ASSOC OF ROVER CLUBS LTD, 10 Highfield Road, Bagslate, Rochdale OL11 5RZ

P.H.J. Whyman, ASTON MARTIN OC, 1A High Street, Sutton, Nr Ely, Cambs. EB6 2RB

B. Harris, ASTRA MC, 71 West Street, Sittingbourne, Kent, ME10 1AN

T. Westhall, AUSTIN TEN DC LTD, 21 Kellynch Close, Alton, Hants. GU34 2EG

Mrs L. Heathcote, AUSTIN HEALEY CLUB NORTHERN, The White House, Alderdale Drive, High Lane, Stockport, Cheshire SK6 8BX

T. Moore, AUSTIN HEALEY CLUB MIDLANDS, 129 Montague Road, Rugby, Warwickshire, CV22 6LQ

G. Franks, AUSTIN HEALEY CLUB (SC), Leighbridge Farm, Hawkenbury, Nr Staplehurst, Headcorn, Kent

Mrs C. Marks, AUSTIN HEALEY CLUB LTD (SW), 171 Coldharbour Road, Bristol BS6 7SX

T. Elshof, AUSTIN HEALEY CLUB (NAT), Trinity Court, Trinity Street, Bungay, Suffolk

J.A.T. Halls, AUSTIN HEALEY CLUB (EASTERN), 147 Briar Road, Kingswood, Watford, Herts. WD2 6HL

A.J. Swann, AUSTIN CAMB WESTMINSTER CC, 21 Alexander Terrace, Corsham, Wiltshire SN13 0BW

D.J. Coates, AUTOTEST DC NI LTD, 11 Alandale, Bangor, Co Down, Northern Ireland BT19 2DF

P.M. Hillaby, AUTO 66 CLUB, New Road, Nafferton, Driffield, Nth Humberside

Mr Maldwyn Jones, AUTOMOBILE C NORTH WALES, Tan-y-coed, Valley Rd, Llandfarfechan, Gwynedd

D.H. Penny, AVON (BRADFORD) MC, 16 Clarendon Road, Trowbridge, Wiltshire BA14 7BR

M. Wise, AYLESBURY MC, 6 Como Road, Aylesbury, Bucks HP20 INR

B. Tremlett (PB249), BACMC, British Aerospace, Six Hills Way, Stevenage, Herts. SG1 2DA

Tony Bowher, B.A.D. CLUB, The Flat, 2 Castle Street, Worksop, Notts. S80 1LH

D. Watkins Edwards, BALA DMC, Post Office, High Street, Bala LL23 7AB

N.D. Luke, BARCLAYS BANK MC (SW), 12 St Marys Park, Ottery St Mary, Devon EX11 1JA

S.A. Mynott, BARCLAYS BANK MC (LONDON), 32 Highfields Mead, East Hanningfield, Chelmsford, Essex CM3 8XA

R.P. Whitehead, BARCLAYS BANK MC (LEEDS), 45 Grange Road, Eldwick, Bingley, West Yorks BD16 3DQ

J. Leck, BARC (NW), 30 Glendyke Road, Liverpool, Merseyside L18 7JR

P.J. Goodhead, BARCLAYS BANK MC, 20 Egerton Road, Streetly, Sutton Coldfield, West Midlands B74 3PQ

J.M. English, BARC (YORKSHIRE), 32 Farfield Avenue, Knaresborough, North Yorks. HG5 8HB

D.J. Goldthorpe, BARCLAYS BANK MC PRESTON, Barclays Bank plc, 13 Marine Road West, Morecambe, Lancs.

Mr R.M. Norris, BARC (LONDON & HOME COUNTIES), 24 Artington Walk, Guildford, Surrey GU2 5EA

G.E. Taggart, BARCLAYS BANK MC MANCHESTER, 2 Elleray Road, Alkrington, Middleton, Manchester M24 1NY

D.E.J. Wort, BARC (SOUTH WESTERN), 16 Bond Road, Bitterne Park, Southampton SO2 4LP

Mrs H.A. Mead, BASINGSTOKE MOTOR CLUB, Grammarsham House, Farleigh, Wallop, Basingstoke RG25 2HW

B. White, BATH UNIV MC, Motor C C-O Students Union, Bath University, Claverton Down, Bath BA2 7AY

R. Pease, BATH MC LTD, 85 Leigh Park Road, Bradford on Avon, Wiltshire BA15 1TG

Mrs Y. Tramm, BRITISH DRAG RACING ASSOC, Bakersfield, 29 West Drive, Caldecote, Cambs. CB3 7NY

A. Childs, BECCLES & DKC, Oceans Gift Low Road, Thrulton, Norwich, Norfolk NR14 6RL

C.P. Birdsall, BEDFORD CC LTD, 34 The Maples, Stevenage Road, Hitchin, Herts. SG4 9HA

W.J. Port, BENTLEY DC LTD, 16 Chearsley Road, Long Crendon, Aylesbury, Bucks. HP18 9AW

Mr M. Garnett, BENTLEY MC, 38 Littler Lane, Winsford, Cheshire CW7 2NF

A. Bainbridge, BERWICK & DMC, 2 Windmill Hill, Cheswick, Berwick upon Tweed

Ms S. Etherington, BEVERLEY & DMC LTD, 73 Swinemoor Lane, Beverley, North Humberside HU17 0LY

Mr M. Nutt, BEXLEY LCC LTD, 67 Bournewood Road, Orpington, Kent BR5 4JW

Miss V. Knott, BIRMINGHAM UNIV MC, 'Sticklford', Higher Tincleton, Dorchester, Dorset DT2 8QP

Mike Topp, BIRMINGHAM WHEELS KRC, 46 Standedge, Wilnecote, Tamworth, Staffs B77 4LB

I. Jones, BISHOP AUCKLAND MSC, 15 Crawford Close, Bishop Auckland, Co Durham DL14 6PS

Miss M.D. Arnfield, BLACKFRIARS MC, Unilever House, Blackfriars, London EC4P 4BQ

A. McCann, BLACKMILL & DMC, 112 Ewenny Road, Bridgend, Mid Glamorgan

W.S. Cook, BLACKPALFREY MC OF KENT, 23 Alkham Road, Maidstone, Kent ME14 5PA

J. Chapman, BLACKFYNE MC LTD, 12 Hillgarth, Castleside, Consett, Co Durham DH8 9QD

Mrs S. Scott, BLACKBURN WELFARE SOC MC, 13 Old Mill Close, Market Weighton, York YO4 3DU

Rick Kellett, BLACKROD MOTOR CLUB, 270 Breightmet Fold Lane, Red Bridge Park, Bolton, Lancs. BL2 5NB

R.J. Kane, BLYTH VALLEY MC, 25 The Fairway, Loansdean, Morpeth, Northumberland NE61 2DS

Ms E. Corley, BMW CC (GB) LTD, 558 London Road, Isleworth, Middlesex TW7 4EP

Mrs B. Wadge, BOGNOR REGIS MC, 42 Gossamer Lane, Aldwick, Bognor Regis PO21 3BZ

E. Price, BOLTON KC, 26 Walnut Street, Bolton BL1 8LN

Mr G.S. Darcy, BOLTON LE MOORS CC LTD, 8 Frome Close, Astley, Tyldesley, Gtr Manchester M29 7NP

T.K. Withell, BOOTS MC, The Boots Co plc, CPD D98, Nottingham NG2 3AA

G. Brautigam, BORDER MC (FINNINGLEY), 13 Rands Lane, Armthorpe, Doncaster, South Yorks

Mr N. Halcrow, BORDER ECOSSE CC LTD, 6 The Loaning, Whitsome, Duns, Berwickshire TD11 3NA

D. Wilkins, BOROUGH 19 MC, 27 Glebelands, Iron Mill Lane, Crayford, Kent DA1 4RY

S.B.J. Brooks, BOROUGH 18 MC, 23 Westway, Shirley, Croydon, Surrey CR0 8RQ

D.J. Minns, BOSTON & DMC & LCC, Yew Tree Farm, Frampton West, Boston, Lincs PE20 1RX

Mr A. Bergin, BOURNEMOUTH & DCC, 5 Saxonhurst Close, Northbourne, Bournemouth, Dorset BH10 6LL

Angela Dowsett, BRANDS HATCH LEISURE RC, Brands Hatch Circuits Ltd, Fawkham, Nr Dartford, Kent DA 38NG

Mike Stapleton, BRECKLAND LRC LTD, The Old Post Office, 2 South Street, Hockwood-cum-Wilton, Norfolk

Mrs C. Price, BRECON MC, 63 Beechgrove, Brecon, Powys LD3 9ET

Miss S. Ayley, BRENT VALE MC, 128 Woodrow Ave, Hayes, Middx. VB4 8QP

T. Pedersen, BRIDGEND AC LTD, 98 Millfield Drive, Cowbridge, S. Glamorgan CF7 7BR

Miss E.J. Bough, BRIDLINGTON AND DMC, 59 Jewison Lane, Bridlington, North Humberside YO15 1DX

T. Johnstone, BRIGHTON & HOVE MC, 22 Braybon Avenue, Patcham, Brighton BN1 8EA

A.J. Streeting, BRISTOL MC & LCC, Nevasa, Highfields, Hawkesbury, Upton, Badminton, Avon GL9 1BJ

D.B. Taylor, BRISTOL AEROPLANE CO MC, Flat 7, 6 Victoria Walk, Cotham, Bristol

Lt Col (RETD) E.P. Bartlett, BRITISH ARMY MOTORING ASSOC, Normandy Barracks, Leconfield, N. Humberside LU17 7LX

Mrs. S.R. Knight, BRIT TRIAL & RALLY DRV ASSN, Litfield House, 15 Cabstand Portishead, Bristol BS20 9H

L.D. Pullen, BRITISH RACING DRIVERS CLUB, BRDC Silverstone Circuit, Silverstone, Towcester, Northants NN12 8TN

M. Poynton, BRITISH AUTOMOBILE RC, Thruxton Circuit, Andover, Hants SP11 8PN

Mrs C. Taylor, BRITISH KC, Bank House, Summerhill, Chislehurst, Kent BR7 5RD

Miss J. Thwaites, BRITISH WOMEN RDC, 151 Lordship Lane, East Dulwich, London SE22 8HX

K.B. James, BRIT MOTOR RACING MARSHALS, 2 Temple Close, Bletchley, Milton Keynes MK3 7RG

G.M. Webb, BRITISH RALLYCROSS DRV ASN, 11 Swan Lane, Stock, Essex CM4 9BQ

Mrs Margaret Coe, BRITISH RALLY MARSHALS CLUB, 26 Launde Park, Little Bowden, Market Harborough, Leics.

Roger Sparshatt, BRITISH TRUCK RACING ASSO, Sparshatts of Kent Ltd, Unit 10, Eurolink Ind Est, Sittingbourne ME10 3RN

S.A. Forster, BROMBOROUGH POOL MC, 16 Langley Close, Spital, Wirral, Merseyside L63 9YN

Mrs S. Ogden, BROMSGROVE KC LTD, 28 Montreal Close, Lower Wick, Worcester WR2 4DZ

P.G. Dench, BROOKLANDS SOCIETY LTD, Reigate Lodge, Chart Way, Reigate, Surrey RH2 0NZ

Howard Gittins, BROUGHTON & BRETTON MC, Garinish, Harwoods Lane, Rossett, Wrexham

J. Nicol, BRITISH RACING & SPORTS CC, Brands Hatch Circuit, Fawkham, Dartford, Kent DA3 8NH

E. Goodman, BRSCC EAST ANGLIA, 55 Arran Road, Catford, London SE6 2LT

T.K. Dooley, BRSCC NW CENTRE, 285 Brooklands Road, Manchester M23 9HF

R.D. Llewelyn, BRSCC (SW), 16 Pilgrims Way, Downend, Bristol BS16 6JW

Mrs E. Wright, BRSCC NORTH, 17 Parkstone Grove, Leeds LS16 6EX

E.B. Smart, BRSCC (MIDLAND), 9 Hadstock Close, Sandiacre, Nottingham NG10 5LQ

G.W.G. Ward, BUGATTI OC LTD, Prescott Hill, Gotherington, Cheltenham, Glos. GL52 4RD

Ms L. Woodward, BURMAH CASTROL MOTOR CLUB, Burmah Castrol UK Ltd, Burmah House, Pipers Way, Swindon SN3 1RE

Mrs S. House, BURNHAM ON SEA MC, 32 Bushy Coombe Gardens, Glastonbury, Somerset BA6 8JT

C.P. Mansley, BURY AC, 9 Cox Green Road, Egerton, Bolton BL7 9HF

J.H. Shaw, CADWELL C & KC, Armdale, Armtree Road, Langrick, Nr Boston, Lincs. PE22 7AQ

P.J. Roberts, CAERNARVONS & ANGLESEY MC, Ffrwd Galed, Tregarth, Bangor, Gwynedd LL57 4PL

Mr I. Macdonald, CAITHNESS CC LTD, 80 Duncan Street, Thruso, Caithness

D. Grogan, CALDERDALE MC, 57 Fore Lane Avenue, Beechwood, Sowerby, Halifax HX6 1BB

L. Jackson, CAMBERLEY KC, 61 Willow Crescent West, New Denham, Uxbridge, Middx UB9 4AU

A. Cole, CAMBRIDGE KC, 30 Stormont Road, Hitchin, Herts. SG5 1SH

Matthew Schumann, CAMBRIDGE UNIV. AC, Trinity Hall, Cambridge CB2 1TJ

C.S. Grounds, CAMBRIDGE CC LTD, 19 Youngman Avenue, Histon, Cambridge CB4 4HP

Mr P. Wellington, CAMEL VALE MC, Pengarth, St. Giles Drive, Wadebridge, Cornwall PL27 6DJ

Brian Owen, CANNOCK AND DCC, 50 St. Pauls Road, Burntwood, Walsall WS7 0DG

Mrs V. Williams, CARDIFF KC, Doghill Farm, St. Nicholas, Nr Cardiff, S. Glam. CF5 6SU

V. Orme, CARLTON AND D MC LTD, 41 Ribblesdale Road, Long Eaton, Nottingham NG10 3JH

Mr D.G. Rees, CARMARTHEN MC, 5 Spring Gardens, Carmarthen, Dyfed SA31 3LL

I. Rushforth, CENTRAL KC, 11 Sunny Grove, New Costessey, Norwich, Norfolk NR5 0EJ

Mrs K. Capsey, CENTRAL SUSSEX MC, Lyne Farm, Capel, Dorking, Surrey RH5 5HG

Miss G.M. Mills, CHASEWATER KRC, 3 Morgan Road, Fazeley Road, Tamworth, Staffs. B78 3LA

D. Cooper, CHELTENHAM MC, Cheltenham Motor Club, Priory Lawn, London Road, Cheltenham, Glos.

N. Booth, CHELMSFORD MC, 52 Ashley Green, East Hanningfield, Chelmsford Essex CM3 8AY

I. Williams, CHESTER MC LTD, 4 Parkfield Drive, Whitby, Ellesmere Port, Cheshire L65 6SN

M.W. Hughes, CHESTER VINTAGE EC, 33 Farndon Way, Oxton, Birkenhead, Merseyside L43 2NW

Andrew Guttridge, CHESS VALLEY MC, 9 Newtown, Codicote, Hichin, Herts. SG4 8UG

T.H. Rowe, CHESHIRE CATS CC, 11 Fairview Road, Timperley, Cheshire WA15 7AR

G.R. Glazebrook, CHESHIRE KC LTD, 107 West Vale, Little Neston, South Wirral L64 0SF

A. Britwell, CHILTERN CC, 28 Rushmoor Avenue, Hazlemere, High Wycombe, Buckinghamshire HP15 7NP

P. Lawrence, CIRENCESTER CC LTD, 52 Down View, Chalford Hill, Stroud, Gloucestershire GL6 8NB

B. Drummond, CITROËN CC, 5 Bishops Close, Hurstpierpoint, West Sussex BN6 9XU

Mr T.J. Clark, CITY & GUILDS COLLEGE MC, City & Guilds C/U Mech Dpt., Imperial College, London SW7 2BX

Mr R.P. Crewe, CLASSIC & HISTORIC MC LTD, 103A Station Road, Clutton, Nr Bristol

K.D. Mumford, CLASSIC TRIALS DC, 18 Dane Close, Gwersyllt, Wrexham, Clywd LL11 4SJ

Mrs P. Newsham, CLAY PIGEON KART CLUB LTD, 257 Preston Road, Yeovil, Somerset

Mrs J.P. Bateson, CLITHEROE & DMC, 10 Barleydale Road, Barrowford, Nr Nelson, Lancs. BB9 6AD

Mr S. Ashley, CLOWNE & DMC, 39 Morven Street, Creswell, Worksop, Notts. S80 4AJ

V. Adaway, CLUBMANS REGISTER, 70 Nest Lane, Wellingborough, Northants NN8 4AX

D.A. Pollock, CLUB TRIUMPH (NORTH LONDON), 86 Waggon Road, Hadley Wood, Herts. EN4 0PP

P.M. Cross, CLUB TRIUMPH (WORCS), 6 Summervale Road, Hagley, Stourbridge, West Midlands DY9 0LY

R. Budd, CLUB TRIUMPH (WARKS), 54 Shirlett Close, Coventry CV2 1PG

M. Warren, CLUB TRIUMPH LTD, 14 John Simpson Close, Wolston, Coventry CV8 3HX

David Tydeman, CLUB TRIUMPH (EASTERN), 12 Elderton Road, Westcliff on Sea, Essex

J. Gillo, CLWB MODUR CYMRU, Mailscot, 67 Primrose Way, Lydney, Glos. GL15 5SQ

G.W. Jones, CLWYD VALE MC, 24 Snowdon Avenue, Bryn Y Baal, Mold, Clwyd CH7 6SZ

Mr Rob Dyson, COALVILLE CC, Wayside Cottage, The Common, Peckleton, Leicester LE9 7RF

H. Bailey, COELBREN AND DMC, 251 Clydach Road, Morriston, Swansea SA6 9AJ

D. Graham, COLERAINE & DMC, 41 Hartford Park, Ballysally, Coleraine N I

Mr T. Hamill, COLERAINE & DMC KS, 92 Newmills Road, Coleraine, Northern Ireland

Ms A. Cavanagh, COLTNESS CC LTD, 38 Hyndford Road, Lanark ML11 9AE

A. Ivens, COMBINED ONEMAKE CC, 51 Melbourne Way, Enfield, Middx EN1 1XG

I. Giboney, COOKSTOWN AND DMEC, 4 Fairhill Close, Cookstown, Co Tyrone BT80 8DH

David J. Marsh, CORNWALL & DEVON LROC, 23 Springfield Road, Plynstock, Plymouth, Devon PL9 8EB

Elizabeth Hill, CORNWALL VINTAGE V/S, 35 Tresawls Avenue, Truro, Cornwall

K. Bradley, COSMOPOLITAN CC LTD, 1 Bedhampton Road, North End, Portsmouth, Hants. PO2 YJX

K.D. Sheather, COTSWOLD MOTOR SPORT GROUP, 204 Old Bath Road, Cheltenham, Glos. GL53 9EQ

J. Roberts, COTSWOLD MS GROUP CC, 9 Catkin Close, Quedgeley, Glos. GL2 6XS

Mrs L. Stephens, COVENTRY & WARWICKSHIRE MC, 47 New Street, Cubbington, Leamington Spa CV32 7LA

Gary Waite, COVENTRY POLYTECHNIC MC, Coventry Polytechnic Students Union, Priory Street, Coventry

D.W. Wilson, CRAMLINGTON & DMC, 31 Fairways Avenue, Benton, Newcastle upon Tyne

N.J. Wilmshurst, CRANE VALLEY MC, 39 Warley Avenue, Hayes, Middx. UB4 0RA

B. Ambler, CRANLEIGH MC, 4 Harrier Close, Cranleigh, Surrey GU6 7BS

Ms S. Stapleton, CRAVEN MC LTD, 27 Ennerdale, Bracknell, Berks. RG12 4RT

Ms T. Best, CRAWLEY MC, 11 The Gattons, Burgess Hill, Crawley, Sussex

T. Large, CROYDON & DMC LTD, 2 Cheriton Court, 107 Burnt Ash Hill, London SE12 0AR

C.N. Devenish, CIVIL SERVICE MOTORING ASSN, CSMA Brittannia House, 95 Queens Road, Brighton BN1 3WY

S. Leak, CSMA (WESSEX & SW) LTD, Woodcroft, Willsbridge, Bristol BS15 6EJ

P. Grohmann, CSMA (SOUTH LONDON) LTD, 41 Coleridge Way, Orpington, Kent BR6 0UQ

H. Kelly, CSMA (SOUTHERN) LTD, 161 Coombe Vale Rd, Teignmouth, Devon TQ14 9ER

N. Jennings, CSMA (SOUTH EAST) LTD, 313 Wigmore Road, Gillingham, Kent ME8 0LU

C. Jones, CSMA (SCOTTISH) LTD, Top Flat, Brighton House, Temple Street, Llandrindod Wells, Powys

S. Johnson, CSMA (NORTH WEST) LTD, 9 Aitken Street, Accrington, Lancs. BB5 6AX

M. Biss, CSMA (NORTH LONDON) LTD, 6 Wavertree Road, South Woodford, London E18

K. Baglee, CSMA (NORTHERN) LTD, 'Orinoco', Stainton, Penrith, Cumbria CA11 0ET

G. Davis, CSMA (MIDLANDS & STH WALES), 39 Kenwood Avenue, Worcester WR4 9BL

T. Kirby, CSMA (EAST MIDLANDS) LTD, 8 Forsythia Close, Branston, Lincoln LN4 1PS

P. Holmes, CSMA (EAST ANGLIA) LTD, Paddock Hill, Grundisburgh Rd, Gt Bealings, Woodbridge, Suffolk IP13 6PE

C. Pratt, CSMA (CENTRAL SOUTHERN) LTD, 21 Egremont Drive, Jason Heights, Lower Earley, Reading, Berks. RG6 3BS

D. Smith, CSMA (YORKSHIRE) LTD, 20 Hodgson Lane, Drighlington, Bradford, West Yorks.

P. Anstiss, CUMBRIAN ROC, 4 Bluecoat Crescent, Newton with Scales, Preston, Lancashire PR4 3TJ

Mr T. Yates, CUMBERLAND SPORTING CC, 68 Lansdowne Crescent, Stanwix Carlisle CA3 9EP

Mr Michael Harvey, CUMBRIA KRC, South Farm, Celleron, Nr Penrith, Cumbria CA10 2LS

P. Riley, CUMBRIA MSG, 31 Ennerdale Drive, Barrow-in-Furness, Cumbria

B. Thorne, DAIMLER & LANCHESTER OC LTD, Rivermede, Paynes Green, Ockley, Surrey RH5 5NH

A. Stout, DARLINGTON & DMC LTD, 3 Staffordshire Drive, Moor Park, Belmont, Durham DH1 2DW

R.T. Williams, DAVID BROWN S&S CMS, 2 Spring Lane, Holmfirth, Huddersfield HD7 1LN

Mr G. Round, DE LACY MC LTD, 5 Micklewaite View, Wetherby, West Yorks. LS22 5HB

Doug Phillips, DEUX CHEVAUX CLUB OF GB, 45 Watford Road, Crick, Northampton NN6 7TT

C. Jones, DEVIZES DMC LTD, Partacre, Horton, Carsham, Devizes, Wilts SN10 3NB

N.C. Turner, DOLPHIN MC (NEWBURY), 36 Enborne Road, Newbury, Berks. RG14 6AH

Glynis Limb, DONINGTON RC, Donington Park, Castle Donington, Derby DE7 2RP

Mrs W. Evans, DOVEY VALLEY MC, Tegfan, Brickfield Street, Machynlleth, Powys

J. Davis, DOWTY MC, Cad Dept, Dowty Rotol Ltd, Cheltenham Road East, Gloucester GL2 9QH

Mr A.V. Bourn, DROOP SNOOT GROUP, 41 Horsham Avenue, Finchley, London N12 9BG

Ms J. Faragher, DRUIDALE MC, 20 Victoria Ave, Onchan, Isle of Man

A.K. Wright, DUKERIES MC LTD, 305 Southwell Road West, Mansfield, Nottinghamshire

A. Foubister, DUNFERMLINE CC LTD, 102 Craigcrook Road, Edinburgh EH4 3PN

J.R.E. Beatty, DUNGANNON MC LTD, 68 Killyman Road, Dungannon, Co Tyrone, Northern Ireland BT71 6DG

Mrs D.L. Mitchell, DUNKESWELL KRC LTD, 68C Deane Drive, Galmington, Taunton, Somerset TA1 5PR

C.M.C. Griffiths, DUNLOP MC B'HAM, 720 Walsall Road, Great Barr, Birmingham B42 1EX

D. Rammson, DURHAM UNIV MC, DUMC, St Cuthberts Society, 12 South Bailey, Durham DH1 3EE

S. Simpkins, DURHAM AC LTD, 11 The Close, Lanchester, Durham

R.J. Tillott, EAST GRINSTEAD MC, 11 Bracken Close, Copthorne, Crawley, West Sussex RH10 3QE

Mr Barker, EAST FIFE MC, South Cottage, West Lodge, Kilrie by Kirkcaldy, Fife

Mrs J. McMillan, EAST AYRSHIRE CC LTD, Laurelbank House, 1 Alloway Road, Maybole, Ayrshire

P.A. Lyon, EAST ELLOE MC LTD, 89 Back Gate, Cowbit Spalding, Spalding, Lincs. PE12 6AP

G. Leeson, EASTERN COUNTIES MC, 46 Gosford Way, Felixstowe, Suffolk

Mrs S. Hickling, EASTWOOD & DMC, 18 Philip Ave. Nuthall, Notts. NG16 1EA

Mrs S.J. Lower, EASTBOURNE AND RAM MC, 3 Stafford Road, Seaford, East Sussex BN25 1UF

Wendy Arnold, EAST DEVON OFF ROAD CLUB, Birch House, Clayhidon, Cullompton, Devon EX1 53PH

Mr Steve Mitchell, EAST MIDLANDS OFF ROAD CL, 23 Spring Gardens, Newark, Notts. NG24 4UW

Ms Kath Barber, ECURIE ROYAL OAK MC LTD, 71 Tidnock Avenue, Congleton, Cheshire CW7 2HN

P. Nicholson, EDEN VALLEY MC, 10 Murton Close, Appleby in Westmorland, Cumbria CA16 6RE

Peter Trace, EDINBURGH UNIV MC, c/o 48 The Pleasance, Edinburgh EH8 9TJ

A. Ivens, EIGHT CLUBS LTD, 51 Melbourne Way, Bush Hill Park, Enfield, Middx.

N. Telfer, EMCOS, 138 Lower Meadows, Quedgley, Glos.

Mrs H. Ogle, ENNISKILLEN MC LTD, Craghan Road, Ballinamallard, Co Fermanagh, N. Ireland

J. Kent, ENTERPRISE AC, 39 Caling Croft, New Ash Green, Kent DA3 8PX

M.J. Probert, EPYNT MC, 26 Brecon Road, Builth Wells, Powys

D.E. Bygrave, ESSEX LAND ROVER OC, Chalkmans Knoll, Bygrave Road, Ashwell, Nr. Baldock, Herts. SG7 5RH

Mrs J. Brundle, ESSEX LADIES MC, 30 Nicholson Crescent, South Benfleet, Essex SS7 1RN

J. Bird, EVESHAM MC LTD, 25 Loughmill Road, Pershore, Worcestershire WR10 1QB

M.R. Edworthy, EXETER MC LTD, 19 Primrose Way, Crediton, Devon EX17M 1BZ

Mr P. Barnard, EXMOUTH MC LTD, 1 Pinn Cottages, Pinn, Sidmouth, Devon EX10 0NN

R.B.B. Gibbs, FAIRTHORPE SCC, Rose Cottage, Hollington, Long Crendon, Bucks. HP18 9EF

J.R. Prestage, FALCON MC, 267 Berecroft, Harlow, Essex CM18 7SQ

K. Martin, FARNBOROUGH DMC, 23 Fintry Walk, Farnborough Hants.

G.N.F. Browning, FED OF BRITISH POLICE MC, Glenallen, Birmingham Road, Allesley, Coventry, Warks CV5 9BA

G.J. Milburn, F.B.P.M.C. West Yorkshire, 11A Highmoor Lane, Hartshead Moor, Cleckheaton, West Yorkshire BD19 6LW

Sally Wildman, FERNIE CC, 9 Hyde Close, Oadby, Leicester LE2 5UN

K. Bradshaw, FERRARI OC LTD, 231 Station Road, Balsall Common, Warwickshire CV7 7EG

P. Phillips, FIAT MC GB, 7 Rosedale Gardens, Walwats Court, Trowbridge, Wiltshire BA14 9TL

Mr P. Ward, FIAT TWIN CAM REGISTER, 59A Poplar Road, Ashford, Middlesex TW15 1EJ

Miss S. Donaldson, FIFTY FIVE CC LTD, 'Cruachan', 21 Polinard, Comrie, Perthshire PH6 2HJ

D.G. Docherty, FIVE HUNDRED OWNERS ASSOC, 68 Upton Park, Chester, CH2 1DQ

Mrs W. Parke, 500 MRC OF IRELAND, 2B Mount Merrion Avenue, Belfast, BT6 0AX N. Ireland

F.C.J. Weir, 500 MRCI LTD (KARTING SEC), 124 Mountstewart Road, Carrowdore, Newtownards, Co Down, BT22 2ES

H. Fisher, FORD RS OC, 44 Coleridge Road, Crouch End, London, N8 8ED

S. Wade, FORD AVO OWNERS CLUB, 43 Hampden Close, North Weald, Essex

J. Colyer, FORD 105E OC, Ambercot, Copperfield Drive, Leeds, Maidstone, Kent ME17 1SY

Robert Watt, FORD ESCORT 1300E O.C., 55 Lindley Road, Walton-on-Thames, Surrey KT12 3EZ

P.C. Turley, FOREST OF DEAN MC LTD, Heathmount, Woodside Bream, Lydney, Glos.

I.A. Smith, FORMULA E ASSOCIATION, 7 Thirsk Close, Runcorn, Cheshire WA7 4YY

W.A. Cartwright, FORRESTERS CAR CLUB, 16 Tewkesbury Walk, Newport, Gwent NP9 5HP

Mr C.D. Stevens, 432 SOLIHULL MC LTD, 19 Kingswood Road, West Heath, Birmingham B31 4RR

A.R. Mitchell, FRAZER NASH SECTION VSCC, Carpenter Cottage, Clee St. Margaret, Craven Arms, Shropshire

Miss Charlotte Godfrey, FURNESS DMC LTD, 2 Burlington Close, Kirkby in Furness, Cumbria

Mr A.P. Duckworth, GARSTANG & DMC, 12 Silsden Ave, Preston, Lancs. PR2 6XB

I. Thompson, GINETTA OC, 82 Rectory Close, North Yate, Bristol BS17 5SE

J. Rintoul, GLENROTHES MSC LTD, Karnuke, Bridgend Ceres, Cupar, Fife KY15 5LS

Ms S. Cobb, GLOSSOP & DCC, 10 Worcester Grove, Glossop, Derbyshire SK13 8SJ

Mrs R. Isacc, GRAMPIAN KART CLUB, East Cottage, North Footie, Torphins, Banchory AB3 4JE

R. Warne, GREEN BELT MC, 9 Chandlers Way, Hertford, Hertfordshire SG14 2EB

Colin Jebson, GRIMSBY MC LTD, 12A Mulberry Close, Keelby, Grimsby, Humberside DE37 8EX

Mrs V. Le Page, GUERNSEY MCCC, Ortac Retot Lane, Castel, Guernsey, Channel Islands

Mrs H. Robilliard, GUERNSEY K & MC, Bacchus, Clos des Sablons, Sandy Lane, L'Islet, St Sampsons, Guernsey, C.I.

J.G. Doggart, GUERNSEY OLD CAR CLUB, Delamere House, Les Canus, St Sampsons, Guernsey, C.I.

M. Feeney, GUILDFORD MC, 71 Carfax Avenue, Tongham, Farnham, Surrey GU10 1BD

C. Morris, GWENDRAETH VALLEY MC, 2 Velindre Cottage, Mynydd y Garreg, Kidwelly, Dyfed SA17 4LW

Mr J. Dobie, HADRIAN MS LTD, 18 Holderness Rd. St. Gabriels Estate, Newcastle upon Tyne NE6 5RH

Mrs J.A. Clarke, HAGLEY AND DLCC, 462 Groveley Lane, Rednal, Birmingham B45 8UR

D. Joll, HALDON MC LTD, Moorhouse Farm, Bovey Tracey, Devon TQ13 9NT

P. Keel, HAMPTON AND DMC LTD, 185 London Road, Twickenham, Middlesex TW1 1EJ

W.A. Bonney, HANTS & BERKS MC, 282 London Bridge Road, Woodley, Reading, Berks. RG5 4BE

Colin Gross, HANTS & BERKS ROVER OC, 16 Thurlstone Road, Ruislip, Middx. HA4 0BS

Steve Little, HANTS VW OWNERS CLUB, 16 Nordick Gardens, Hedge End, Southampton

Ms M. Rhiannon Jones, HARLECH AND DMC, 9 Glanmorfa Terrace, Tremadog, Porthmadog, Gwynedd LL49 9RW.

Mrs K. Sizeland, HARROW CC LTD, 27 Nethercourt Avenue, Finchley, London N3 1PS

Mrs M. Terry, HART MC, 6 Bartock Close, Brighton Hill, Basingstoke, Hampshire RG22 4DT

Ms E. Broadbent, HARTLEPOOL AND DISTRICT MC, 2 Greystone Cottages, Queensberry Ave, Hartlepool, Cleveland TS26 9NW

Mr A. Reading, HARWELL MOTOR CLUB, 52 Hiskins, Park Farm, Wantage, Oxon OX12 9HU

Mr D. Webb, HASTINGS 1066 AND E SUSSEX, Clearways, St. Johns Rd., Bexhill, Sussex

P.R. Adams, HATFIELD POLY CC, Students Union, PO Box 109, Hatfield Polytechnic, Hatfield, Herts.

B. Thomson, HAWICK & BORDER CC, 10 Livesey Terrace, Penicuik, Mid Lothian EH26 0NA

D.A. Howells, HEADS OF THE VALLEY AC, 13 Duffryn Street, Penallta, Ystrad Mynach, Mid Glamorgan CF8 7GJ

Mr D. Finlay, HELENSBURGH MSC, 9 Glennan Gardens, Helensburgh

Mr Peter Lewis, HEREFORDSHIRE MC LTD, 22 Barton Road, Hereford, Herefordshire HR4 0AY

A.C. Green, HERTS COUNTY A & AE C, 195 Park Street Lane, Park Street, St Albans, Hertfordshire AL2 2BA

D.H. Watts, HERTS CONSTABULARY MC, North Watford Traffic Base, Orbital Road, Garston, Hertfordshire WD2 6ER

G.A. Scholey, HEXHAM & DISTRICT MC LTD, Glendalough, Oakwood, Hexham, Northumberland

S. Bradshaw, HIGH WYCOMBE & DMC, 9 Seymour Court Road, Marlow, Buckinghamshire

Ms C. Blanchard, HIGHLAND CC LTD, 41 Balvaird Terrace, Muir of Ord, Ross-Shire

G. Morriss, HIGH MOOR MC OLDHAM, 10 Dover Street, Hamer, Rochdale OL16 2SZ

M.G. Junod, HILLCLIMB & SPRINT ASSOC, 22 Silhill Hall Road, Solihull, W. Mids B91 1JU

Mrs M. Pither, HISTORIC RALLY CAR REGISTER, Droys Court, Witcombe, Gloucester GL3 4TN

B.E. Cocks, HISTORIC SCC, Colharbour, Kington Langley, Wiltshire SN15 5LY

A.G. Kilbey, HODDESDON KC, 33 Kings Place, Buckhurst Hill, Essex IG9 5EA

Mrs J. Moore, HOLSWORTHY MC LTD, Longlands Bungalow, Clawton, Holsworthy, Devon EX22 6QB

T.M. Hazeldine, HORSHAM & DMC & LCC, Laundry Cottage, Muntham, Itchingfield, Horsham, West Sussex RH13 7NH

M. Powell, HUDDERSFIELD MC, 42 Stocksbank Drive, Mirfield, West Yorkshire

Mrs A. Parker, HUNTS KRC LTD, 17 Sandy Close, Wellingborough, Northants NN8 3AY

Miss J. Leyland, IBA MOTOR CLUB, 1BA Crawley Court, Crawley, Winchester, Hampshire SO23 9RB

I.S. Waddington, ILKLEY & DMC, 17 Moseley Wood Green, Cookridge, Leeds LS16 7HA

R. Hunt, IMP CLUB, 1 Benson Close, Bicester, Oxon OX6 7FQ

M.D. Preston, INTER REGISTER CLUB, Clarendon Villa, Gosport Lane, Lyndhurst, Hants.

Mrs D. Rogers, INTERNATIONAL RALLY DRIVERS, 23 De Verdon Avenue, Belton, Loughborough, Leicestershire LE12 9TY

G.C. Rogers, INVADERS MC LTD, 21 Selborne Walk, Tadley, Basingstoke, Hants. RG26 6JU

M. Kenworthy, ISLE OF MAN KR ASSN, 6 Ashlar Drive, Union Mills, Douglas IOM

A. Forman, ISLE OF WIGHT CC LTD, 19 Wilver Road, Newport, IOW PO30 5DX

T.H. Rowe, JAGUAR DC, 11 Fairview Road, Timperley, Cheshire WA15 7AR

B.W. Jones, JAGUAR APPRENTICE MC, 24 Kingsley Crescent, Bulkington, Coventry

T.H. Rowe, THE JAGUAR CAR CLUB LTD, 11 Fairview Road, Timperley, Cheshire WA15 7AR

Mrs E. Le Cornu, JERSEY MC & LCC, Midway, Croix de Bois, Five Oaks, Jersey, CI

T.N. Scott Warren, JERSEY OLD MC, Jardin du Foret, Mont du Ouaisne, St Brelade, Jersey, CI

Ms C. Sanger, JIM RUSSELL RACING DRIVERS, Jim Russell UK Ltd, Donington Circuit, Castle Donington, Derby

M. Smailes, JOWETT CC, 2 Talgarth Road, Norton, Stockton-on-Tees, Cleveland TS20 1LF

M. Melsome-Smith, KEIGHLEY & DMC, 1 Mount Pleasant Court, 11 Mount Pleasant, Ilkley W. Yorks.

N. Bunney, KENDAL & DMC, 11 Castle View, Sedgwick, Nr Kendal, Cumbria, LA8 0JL

K. Minster, KENTISH BORDER CC, 11 Barclay Avenue, Tonbridge, Kent TN10 4LN

Mrs C. Brown, KETTERING & DCC LTD, 8 Cook Close, Rothwell, Kettering, Northants 0536 712259

M.E. Roath, KIDDERMINSTER MCC, 72 Willowfield Drive, Franche, Kidderminster, Worcestershire DY11 5DP

Colin A. Findlay, KILMARNOCK & LOUDOUN CC, 13 Greenan Way, Doonfoot, Ayr KA7 4EJ

A. Wilson, KINGDOM KC, Dunearn, Orchil Road, Menstrie, Stirlingshire

A. Cunnington, KINGS LYNN & DMC LTD, Apple Tree Cottage, Hocklesgate Fleet, Spalding, Lincs. PE12 8LG

M. Whitelock, KIRKBY LONSDALE MC LTD, Heaves Hotel, Nr Kendal, Cumbria LA8 8EF

A. Jones, KNIGHTON MC LTD, Upper Fishpools, Bleddfa Knighton, Powys LD7 1PA

N. Anderton, KNOWLDALE CC LTD, 34 Ramsden Wood Road, Walsden, Todmorden, Lancashire OL14 7UD

Jeff Gray, KNUTSFORD & DMC LTD, 127 Chester Road, Greenbank, Northwich, Cheshire, CW8 4AA

K.A. Whiting, KODAK CC, Kodak Ltd, CPD W160, Headstone Drive, Harrow, Middx. HA1 4TY

J. Batt, LAGONDA CLUB, 49 Ampthill Road, Maulden, Beds MK45 2DH

K. Alcock, LAKELAND HISTORIC CC, Dodds Howe, Crosthwaite, Kendal, Cumbria LA8 8HX

P. Eeles, LAMPETER & DMC, Ordnance Survey, Darkgate BDS, 3 Red Street, Carmarthen, Dyfed SA31 1QL

S. Clink, LANARKSHIRE CC LTD, Southsyde, Woodhead Avenue, Bothwell, Lanarkshire G71 8AR

Mrs B.M. Rees, LANCIA MC LTD, The Old Shire House, Aylton, Ledbury, Herefordshire HR8 2QE

Mr T. Boydell, LANCASHIRE & CHESHIRE ROC, 9 Melverley Drive, Leigh, Lancashire WN7 2HZ

Mrs L. O'Neil, LANCASHIRE & CHESHIRE CC, 15 Palliser Close, Oakwood, Warrington WA3 6RT

Paul Ratcliffe, LANCASHIRE AC, 29 Longsight Road, Holcombe Brook, Bury BL0 9SL

C. Millar, LARNE MC LTD, 14 Arran Gardens, Larne, Co Antrim BT40 2JU

R. Uglow, LAUNCESTON AND N CORNWALL MC, Trecarne Farm, Delabole, Cornwall PL33 9DG

P.H. Deacon, LAW SOCIETY MC, 50 Gainsborough Drive, Ascot, Berks. SL5 8TB

D. Weeks, LEA FRANCIS OC, Greenacre, The Shripple, Winterslow, Wilts.

S. Harris, LEEDS UNIV UNION MC, 81 Woodside View, Burley, Leeds LS4 2QS

Mrs S. Broomfield, LEEDS MC LTD, 125 Parkway Vale, Leeds, Yorkshire LS14 6XE

Christine Hardy, LEICS LRC LTD, Fearn House, 1 Guilford Dr, Wigston Fields, Leics. LE8 1HG

Mrs L.A. West, LIGHTNING MSC, 64 Frobisher Drive, Lytham St Annes, Lancs FY8 2RG

John Barber, LINCOLNSHIRE LOUTH MC LTD, 12 Antrim Way, Scartho, Grimsby, South Humberside DN33 2DL

R. Wells, LINCOLNSHIRE LAND ROVER C, Shepherds Cottage, Horkstow, Barton on Humberside, South Humberside

J. Sanders, LINCOLN MC & CC LTD, 13 Queen Street, Lincoln

Mrs N. Walsh, LINCOLNSHIRE KRC, 43 College Road, Airedale, Castleford WF10 3EF

Mr L. Fowkes, LINDHOLME MSC, 36 Wellington Avenue, North Anston, Sheffield S31 7HE

Mrs H. Fowler, LION KART CLUB LTD, 24 Morton Street, Middleport, Burslem, Stoke on Trent

A. Silver, LIVERPOOL MC LTD, c/o 227 Thomas Lane, Liverpool, Merseyside L14 5NU

R. McCutcheon, LLANDEILO & DMC, 4 Stepney Road, Llandeilo, Dyfed SA19 6LA

Mrs D. Mantle, LLANIDLOES MC LTD, 32 Longbridge Street, Llanidloes, Powys SY18 6AR

N. Williams, LLANDRINDOD MC, Kielder, Court Close, Abermule, Montgomery SY15 6NU

D.D.S. Harvey, LONDON CC, 22 Sutherland House, Marloes Road, London W8 5LG

Mrs B. Cubitt, LONDON KC, 53 Shearwater New Barn, Longfield, Dartford, Kent DA3 7NL

Andrew J. Santon, LONDON & SURREY MINI OC, 88 Barrow Road, Streatham, London SW16 5PG

Mrs S.A. Wood, LONGTON & DMC, 8 Spring Meadow, Clayton Le Woods, Chorley, Lancashire PR5 4UR

G.D. Stewart, LOTHIAN CC (Edinburgh) Ltd, 16 House O'Hill Crescent, Edinburgh, Scotland, EH4 5DH

R. Egger, LOUGHBOROUGH CC LTD, 224 Bradgate Road, Anstey, Leicestershire LE7 7FD

Mr Christopher Wood, LOUGHBOROUGH STUDENTS KRC, AU Offices, Union Building, Ashby Road, Loughborough, Leics.

C. Blyth, LOUGHBOROUGH STUDENTS MC, Loughborough Students Union, Ashby Rd, Loughborough, Leics.

Mr Michael Wilding, LUDLOW CASTLE MC LTD, Parsonage Farm, Rochford, Tenbury Well, Worcs. WR15 8SP

T.C. Walker, MABLETHORPE AND DMC LTD, Copper Beeches, Burgh Road, Orby, Skegness, Lincs.

R.D. Anderson, MACHARS CC LTD, Wigtown Motor Company, Duncan Park, Wigtown DG8 9JD

Mr T. Frayne, MAESTEG & DMC, 61 Bath Road, Morriston, Swansea SA6 7AT

Martin McKenna, MAGHERAFELT AND DMC LTD, 114 Five Mile Straight, Maghera, Co Londonderry, NI

Ms D. Carlin, MAIDEN CITY MC LTD, 61 Prehen Park, Waterside, Londonderry, Northern Ireland

Alison Cornwell, MAIDSTONE & MID KENT MC LTD, 6 Naildown Close, Seabrook, Hythe, Kent

Miss C. Carter, MALDEN & DMC, 51 Minstrel Gardens, Surbiton, Surrey

Mr J.H. Allison, MALTON MC, 1 Stoop Close, Wigginton, York YO3 8WX

Ms J.C. Webster, MANCHESTER VINTAGE CC, 50 Manor Park South, Knutsford, Cheshire WA16 8AJ

Mr N. Woodhead, MANCHESTER & BUXTON KC, 6 Den Lane, Springhead, Oldham, Lancs OL4 4NH

Andrew Holmes, MANX AS LTD, 127 Ballabrodie Drive, Douglas, Isle of Man

The Secretary, MANX INTERNATIONAL RALLY LT, PO Box 129, Regent Street, Douglas, Isle of Man

M.J. Miles, MASERATI CLUB, The Paddock, Old Salisbury Road, Abbotts Ann, Andover, Hants. SP11 7NT

Ms J. Robinson, MATLOCK MC, 4 Valley Close, Lower Pilsley, Chesterfield, Derbyshire

Mrs A. Ashe, MERSEYSIDE KC, 20 Camdale Close, Stockbridge Village, Liverpool L28 3QD

I. James, METROPOLITAN POLICE MC, Arlington House, 83 Worple Road, Wimbledon, London SW19 4JH

B.J.A. Morgan, MGCC (SW), 14 Conygar Close, Clevedon, Avon, BS21 6AP

D.F. Farrar, MGCC (TYNE TEES), Woodstock, Shiney Row, Chester Le Street, Co Durham

D.W. Mickel, MGCC (SCOTTISH), 12 N Saint Andrew Street, Edinburgh, EH2 1HT

Mr R. Sapcote, MGCC (MIDLAND), PO Box 38, Lichfield, Staffordshire WS14 9YB

P. Goodman, MGCC (NW), 36 Deva Close, Poynton, Stockport, Cheshire

D. Hill, MGCC LINCOLNSHIRE, 7 Maple Close, Keeleby, Lincolnshire DN37 8EL

B. Smith, MGCC (DEVON & CORNWALL), Muttram Cottage, 61 Boringdon Hill, Colebrook, Plymouth, Devon PL7 4DL

B. Sidery-Smith, MGCC LTD (SOUTH EAST), 41 Grasmere Way, Byfleet, Surrey KT14 7BY

Roger Latham, MGCC (ANGLIA CENTRE), 4 Netherfield, Thundersley, Essex SS7 1TY

H. Crutchley, MG OCTAGON CC, 36 Queensville Ave, Stafford ST17 4LS

Steven Templeton, MID ANTRIM MC LTD, 32 Gracefield, Gracehill, Ballymena, Northern Ireland

Hugo Manson, MID ANTRIM MC KART SECTION, 39 Ballygowan Road, Kells, Ballymena, N. Ireland

G.S. Keen, MID-CHESHIRE MRC LTD, 3 Riddings Road, Timperley, Altrincham, Cheshire WA15 6BW

B. Stevenson, MID DERBYSHIRE MC LTD, 12 Archer Street, Cotmanhay, Ilkeston, Derbyshire DE7 8JX

S. Jenkins, MIDDLESEX COUNTY AC LTD, 29 Merrivale Mews, Tavistock Road, West Drayton, Middlesex

M.T. Joseland, MIDLAND AC (EST 1901) LTD, Woodbridge, Upper Sapey, Worcester WR6 6EX

P. Oakden, MIDLAND ROC, Oak Cottage, Wood Lane, Norton Juxta Twycross, Atherstone, Warks. CV9 3QB

B.R. Capon, Co Midland Bank, MIDLAND BANK MC, Central Unit Spec Ind. 3rd Floor, 47 Cannon St. London EC4M 5SQ

John Hunt, MIDLAND AUSTIN SEVEN CLUB, 29 Waseley Road, Rubery, Birmingham B45 9TJ

C. Deverill, MIDLAND OFFROAD CLUB, 26 The Cotswolds, Alvechurch Highway, Bromsgrove B60 1PA

Mrs M.D. Rotherham, MIDLAND DRAG RACING ASSO, 214 Alcester Road South, Kingsheath, Birmingham B14 6DE

D. Speer, MID SURREY AC LTD, 5 Effingham Road, Surbiton, Surrey KT6 5JZ

R.A. Scripps, MID-THAMES CC, Stage Two, 18 Shortwood Avenue, Staines, Middx. TW18 5JL

Mr S. Price, MID WIRRAL MC, 51 Springfield Ave, Newton, West Kirkby, Wirral, Merseyside

D. Jones, MILESTONE MC LTD, 21 Bryn Gwyn, Coedpoeth, Nr Wrexham, Clwyd LL11 3PR

Mrs Diane Cook, MILTON KEYNES & DMC, 14 Hastings, Stoney Stratford, Milton Keynes AK11 1EW

L. Woodward, MINEHEAD MC, 8 Larviscombe Road, Williton Taunton, Somerset TA4 4SA

I.D. Jarman, MINI COOPER SPORTS REGISTER, 319 Sutherland Ave, Welling, Kent DA16 2NQ

T. Hall, MINICROSS DRIVERS ASSOC, 48 Firfield Road, Thundersley, Benfleet, Essex SS7 3UU

Peter Tisdale, MINI SEVEN RACING CLUB, 33 Stoke Road, Slough, Berks SL2 5AH

R. Thompson, MONARCH AC LTD, 94 Thimblemill Road, Warley, West Mids. B67 5QU

Miss S. Livingstone, MONOPOSTO RACING CLUB, 2 Juniper Road, Langley Green, Crawley, Sussex RH11 7NL

Mr I. Brown, MORECAMBE CC LTD, 27 The Drive, Crag Bank Carnforth, Lancs.

B. Iles, MORGAN SPORTS CC, Hollands Farm, Coombe Green, Birtsmorton, Malvern, Worcs. WR13 6AB

P. Levett, MORRIS REGISTER, 7 Oak Wood Drive, Barnehurst, Kent DA7 6ED

R. Newell, MORRIS MINOR OC, 84 High Street, Loscoe, Derbyshire DE7 7LF

H.W. Tucker Peake, MOTOR CYCLING CLUB, Upper Stonecroft, Finmere, Nr. Buckingham MK18 4JA

E. O'Donnell, MULL CAR CLUB, 27 Rockfield Road, Tobermory, Isle of Mull

Stuart Higgs, NAIRN AND DMSC, 82 Wyvis Drive, Nairn, Scotland IV12 4TP

N. Howell, NANTWICH DMC, 10 Hatchmere Drive, Great Boughton, Chester CH3 5SE

Mr M. Rumbold, NATIONAL DRAG RA, 61 Chedworth Close, Church Hill, Redditch, Worcs. B98 8QT

John Hill, NATIONAL SCHOOLS KART ASSOC, 51 Stanley Road, Market Bosworth, Nuneaton, Warwickshire

Mr M.I. Fielding, NATIONAL WESTMINSTER BANK MC, 15 Dinorben Close, Fleet, Aldershot GU13 9SL

M.J. James, NAT WEST BANK MC (SOUTH EAST), 24 Manor Close, Canterbury, Kent CT1 3XA

K. Lewis, NAT WEST BANK MC (NOTTS), 110 Station Road, Selston, Nottingham NG16 6FH

D. Graham, NAT WEST BANK MC (LEEDS), 8 Jerwood Hill Close, Horley Green, Halifax, West Yorkshire HX3 6BL

L. Liddle, NEWCASTLE AND DMC, The Lodge, Mount Royal, Allendale Road, Hexham, Northumberland

Mr P.A. Clark, NEWCASTLE UNIVERSITY MC, Newcastle University M/C, Union Society, Kings Walk, Newcastle upon Tyne

N. Fuller, NEWPORT CC LTD, 6 Tennyson Road, Caldicot, Newport, Gwent

D. Kessell, NEWQUAY AC LTD, Whitegate, St Dennis, St Austell, Cornwall PL26 8DT

R. Philpott, NEWRY & DMC LTD, 76 Rugby Road, Belfast, N. Ireland BT7 1PT

Mr D. Nay, NEWTOWN & DAC, 117 Lon Gerylli, Maesy Dail, Newtown Powys

Mrs A. Caswell, NORFOLK & SUFFOLK KC, 9 The Fields, Tacolneston, Norfolk NR16 1DG

J. Graham, NORMANBY & DMC LTD, 25 Ingleby Road, Longlands, Middlesbrough, Cleveland TS4 2JU

Mrs P. McQueen, NORTH OF SCOTLAND KC, 'Stacpolly', 102 Diriebught Road, Inverness IV2 3LT

Mr Stuart Higgs, NORTH EAST OF SCOTLAND MC GROUP, 82 Wyvis Drive, Nairn, Scotland

Mr W. McFetridge, NORTH ULSTER CC LTD, 88 Tobar Park, Cullybackey, Co Antrim BT42 1NN

Mr D.J. Smith, NORTH OXON CC LTD, 49 Daventry Rd, Banbury, Oxon OX16 7JS

N.C. Patterson, NORTHERN BANK MC, 9 Dunmore Park, Troopers Lane, Co Antrim BT36 6LEE

B.S. Turner, NORTH WALES CC LTD, 14 Victoria Park, Colwyn Bay, Clwyd LL29 7AX

Mrs S. Davies, NORTHERN VINTAGE TRANSPORT ASS, 6 Granville Avenue, Hartlepool, Cleveland TS26 8ND

S. Lawson, NORTHERN IRELAND MC LTD, 8 Annaghanoon Road, Waringstown, Craigavon, Co Armagh BT66 7RZ

Miss Helen Broadhead, NORTH DEVON MC, 31 Oak Tree Drive, Westacott Rd, Barnstaple, Devon

Mrs E.A. Hepplewhite, NORTHERN SPORTING TRIALS CC, Farlam Ghyll Hallbankgate, Brampton, Cumbria CA8 2NH

J. Richardson, NORTHALLERTON AC LTD, 255 Ashlands Road, Northallerton, North Yorkshire DL6 1HF

R. Newlove, NORTH HUMBERSIDE MC LTD, Nans Cottage, Orchard Lane, Hutton, Driffield, North Humberside YO25 9PZ

I.M. Campbell, NORTH EASTERN ROC, 29 Beaconsfield Street, Blyth, Northumberland NE24 2DP

Nigel Evans, NORTHAMPTON & DCC LTD, 23 Shepperton Close, Castlethorpe, Milton Keynes, Bucks.

A. Hill, NORTHERN OFF ROAD CLUB LTD, 3 Landsdowne Close, Baildon, W. Yorkshire

M. Allen, NORTH ARMAGH MC & CC LTD, 44 Drumanphy Road, Portadown, Craigavon BT62 1SN

J.R. Davison, NORTHUMBRIAN KC, 6 Valeside, Throckley, Newcastle upon Tyne NE15 9LA

D. Mitchell, NORTH WALES LAND ROVER C, The Steppes, Pen Y Bal Hill, Holywell, Clwyd

Mr D. Cole, NOTTINGHAM SCC, 2 New Cottages, Glen Rd, Newton Harcourt, Leicester LE8 0FH

J. Soars, NUNEATON MC, 4 Linwood Close, Hinckley, Leicestershire LE10 0GX

A. McKane, OMAGH MC LTD, Gortlaoughra, Connaghty Rd, Mountjoy, West Omagh, Co Tyrone, N. Ireland

M.M. Stephenson, ONE-ELEVEN MC, 179 Prospect Road, Bradway, Sheffield S17 4HY

Peter Davis, 182 CLASSIC AND RALLY CLUB, Druidale House, Burton Row, Brent Knoll, Somerset TA9 4BX

John Roberts, 143 MC, 9 Catkin Close, Quedgeley, Glos. GL2 6XS

B. Sneyd, 108 CC, 21 Meadowcroft Sutton, St Helens, Merseyside WA9 3XQ

J. Salmon, ORKNEY MC, Long Reach, Petertown Road, Petertown, Orphir, Orkney, KW7 2RE

A. Turnbull, OTLEY MC LTD, 93 Sandholme Drive, Burnley in Wharfedale, Ilkley, W. Yorkshire LS29 7RG

R. Tolley, OWEN MC LTD, 161 Spies Lane, Halesowen, West Midlands B62 9ST

Mr J. Heath, OXFORD UNIV MDC, St John's College, Oxford

S. Marks, OXFORD MC, 14 Oxford Road, Farmoor, Oxford OX2 9NN

A. Reaney, PEAK & DUKERIES LRC (1983), 96 Ridgeway Road, Gleadless, Sheffield S12 2SY

Miss D. Davies, PEMBROKESHIRE MC LTD, Haywen, 3 Lower Thornton, Milford Haven, Pembrokeshire

Mrs P. Bransten, PENDLE DMC, 3 Long Green, Earby Colne, Lancashire BB8 6RS

P. Dunn, PENINSULA MC, 44 Martins Lane, Wallasey, Wirral L44 1BN

R. Whittaker, PENNINE LRC LTD, 121 Brown Lodge Drive, Smithy Bridge, Littleborough, Lancs. OL15 0ET

Mr Russel Spencer, PENNINE DRAG RC LTD, 61 Coronation Way, Keighley, West Yorkshire

Simon Roberts, PERKINS SAMC, Perkins Engines Ltd, Eastfield, Peterborough PE1 5NA

B. Hill, PETERBOROUGH MC LTD, 67 Exeter Gardens, Stamford, Lincs. PE9 2SA

D.C. Cox, PETERLEE MSC, 33 Brecon Close, Peterlee, Co Durham SR8 2JU

N.R. Maltby, PEUGEOT GTI OC, Peugeot Talbot Motor Co Ltd, PO Box 712, Bickenhill Lane, Birmingham B37 7HZ

Mrs J. Wills, PLYMOUTH KART CLUB, 60 Bridwell Road, Weston Mill, Plymouth PL5 1AB

Mrs S. Sutcliffe, PLYMOUTH KRC LTD, 12 Shallowford Close, Eggbuckland, Plymouth, Devon PL6 5TN

Mrs B.A. Benson, PLYMOUTH MC LTD, Sandpiper Linkadells, Colebrook Plympton, Plymouth, Devon PL7 4EF

Mrs D. Wright, POACHERS MC LTD, 158 Somerby Hill, Grantham, Lincolnshire

Krzysztof Giza, POLISH MOTOR CLUB, 37 Twyford Avenue, London W3 9PZ

K. Drew, PONTYPRIDD AC LTD, 84 Pritchard St, Tonyrefail, Nr Porth, Mid Glamorgan

J. May, PORSCHE C GB, Castle Farm Cottage, Castle Farm, Studley, Warwicks. B80 7AH

D.W. Williams, PORT TALBOT MC LTD, Hafren, 3 Tir Newydd, Llwynhendy, Llanelli, Dyfed SA14 9HW

John Homewood, PORTSMOUTH POLYTECHNIC MC, Alexandra House, Museum Road, Portsmouth PO1 2QH

Mrs S. Brown, PORTALS MC, 24 Heathfield Road, Loddon Vale, Basingstoke, Hants. RG2 24PA

S.O. Griffiths, POTTERIES AND NEWCASTLE MC, 52 Abbots Way, Westlands, Newcastle under Lyme, Staffs. ST5 2EZ

Mrs Y.L. Duncan, PRESTON AC, 19 Freshfields Lea, Preston, Lancs. PR2 1TH

R.J. Brown, PRESTON & D VINTAGE CC, Willow Cottage, 10 Toddy Fold, Pleckgate, Blackburn

Mr D. McCurrie, PRE WAR AUSTIN SEVEN C LTD, 11 Manor Close, Burbage, Hinckley, Leicestershire LE10 2NL

K. Baker, PROPELLERS MC, British Aerospace Dynamics, AW Division, Manor Road, Hatfield AL10 9LL

A. Haley, QUEEN'S UNIV. OF BELFAST MC, Rockville, 22 Warren Road, Donaghadee, County Down BT21 0DT

Mr I. Butcher, QUINTON MC LTD, 61 Sunnybank Road, Sutton Coldfield, West Midlands B73 5RJ

D.N. Mitchell, RANGE ROVER REGISTER LTD, 'The Steppes', Pen-Y-Ball Hill, Holywell, Clwyd CH8 8SZ

Miss C. Cox, READING UNIV. MC, Bridges Hall, Whiteknights Road, Reading, Berkshire RG6 2BG

P.J. Barley, RECKITTS MC, 837 Holderness Road, Hull HU8 9AZ

R. Hollis, REDDITCH & DCC LTD, 6 Tudor Close, Hollywood, West Mids. BT14 4TL

J. Waltho, RED ROSE LRC LTD, 8 Glenmore, Clayton Le Woods, Chorley, Lancs. PR6 7TA

G.W. Cooper, RELIANT SABRE & SCIMITAR OC, 4 Drayton Close, Fetcham Park, Leatherhead, Surrey

P. McMullen, RHYL AND DMC, 39 Glan Ffyddion, Dyserth, Clwyd LL18 6EG

John Sutton, RICARDO MOTOR CLUB, Ricardo Consulting Engs., Bridge Works, Shoreham-by-Sea, West Sussex

Mr Alan Hill, RIPON MSC LTD, 21 Crowgarth, Skelton-on-Ure, North Yorkshire HG4 5AF

P.G. Russell, ROCHESTER MC, 120 Delce Road, Rochester, Kent ME1 2DT

Ms L. Restick, RODING CC, 21 Trent Close, Wickford, Essex SS12 9BW

J. Coupland, ROLLS ROYCE DERBY MC, 2 Foundry Lane, Milford, Derbyshire DE5 0RN

B. Pitcher, ROMFORD ECC, 301 Upper Rainham Road, Hornchurch, Essex RM12 4DB

Rob Gillett, ROSS & DISTRICT MC, Springbank, Brookfield Road, Ross-on-Wye, Herefordshire HR9 7EL

D. Winter, ROTHERHAM MC, 18 Watson Road, Kimberworth, Rotherham, South Yorkshire S61 1JT

H. Dewar, Royal Scottish AC, 11 Blythswood Square, Glasgow, G2 4AG

J. Murray, ROYAL ULSTER CONSTABULARY MC, RUC Station, Strand Road, Londonderry, Co. Londonderry, N. Ireland

Mr J.P. Mead, ROYAL BERKS & HANTS AC, Grammarsham House, Farleigh, Wallop, Basingstoke, Hants. RG25 2HW

Jane Stevenson, RUGBY MC, 41 Wareham Green, Clifford Park, Coventry CV2 2JL

C.J. Wallett, RUGELEY & DMC, 27 Maybank Close, Boley Park, Lichfield, Staffordshire WS14 9UJ

Mrs C.E. Glendinning, RYTON MSC LTD, Lunton Hill, 13 Park Lane, Prudhoe, Northumberland NE42 5LN

J. Broughall, SAAB OC OF GB LTD, Ashburton Cottage, Crampmoor, Romsey, Hampshire SO15 9AL

K. Squire, SAAB MIDLANDS AC, 'Melness', 59 Pooles Lane, Short Heath, Willenheath, West Midlands WV12 5HJ

Mrs J. Aslin, 'SAFETY', Fulford Cottage, Culworth, Banbury, Oxfordshire OX17 2BB

J. Dovey, SALISBURY & SHAFTESBURY CC, 164 Netherhampton Road, West Harnham, Salisbury, Wilts.

Brian Sheridan, SALOON CAR RACING CLUB, 54 Welley Road, Wraysbury, Staines, Middx. TW19 5EP

R. Elliott, SANTA POD RC, 130 Wymington Road, Rushden, Northants.

M.N.C. Gascoigne, SCOT MOTORSPORT MARSHALS C, 24 Barnshot Road, Edinburgh EH13 0DJ

A. Mitchell, SCOTTISH MRC, 25 Market Square, Duns, Berwickshire TD11 3ES

E.A. Tomney, SCOTTISH SPORTING CC, 74 Killermont Road, Bearsden, Glasgow G61 2LS

C.R. Deas, SCOTTISH LAND ROVER OC, 10 Silverburgh Drive, Penicuik, Mid Lothian EH26 9AQ

L. Shelley, SEAXES AC, 1 Tyrells Cottage, Main Road, Boreham, Chelmsford, Essex

B.A. Kilmartin, SELBY & DMC, 5 Chapel Lane, Riccall, York

L. Watson, 750 MC SCOTLAND, 150 Albert Street, Dundee DD4 6QW

D. Bradley, 750 MC LTD, 16 Woodstock Road, Witney, Oxon OX8 6DT

Mrs G. Child, SEVENOAKS & DMC, 4 Hill Close, Chislehurst, Kent BR7 6HY

Mrs F. Adams, SEVERN VALLEY MC LTD, 18 The Parks, Sundorne Grove, Shrewsbury SY1 4TJ

Mr M. Healy, SHEFFIELD AND HALLAMSHIRE, 38 Oakhill Road, Coal Aston, Sheffield

S. Crompton, SHEFFIELD STUDENTS MC, 71 Glencoe Road, Sheffield S2 2SQ

Mrs L. Allen, SHENINGTON KRC, 1 Lisle Gardens, Bishops Tachbrook, Leamington Spa CV33 9QS

C.R. Newton, SHENSTONE & DMC, 4 Hartopp Road, Sutton Coldfield, West Midlands. B74 2RH

G. Weldon, SHIPLEY & DMC LTD, 36 Briarfield Gardens, Shipley, West Yorkshire BD18 2BE

Mrs R. Masters, SILVERSTONE RC, Silverstone Circuit, Nr Towcester, Northants. NN12 8TL

Mr K. Hancock, SILVERTON MC, North Hayes, Knowle Lane, Cullompton, Devon

M. Wray, SINGER OC LTD, 52 Waverley Gardens, Stamford, Lincolnshire PE9 1BH

W. Myron, SIXTY THREE CC (ELGIN) LTD, 59 Duncan Drive, Bishopmill, Elgin Moray IV30 2NG

Janet E. Bennett, SLAITHWAITE MC LTD, 43 Russell Close, Heckmondwike, West Yorkshire WF16 0EG

N. Gowans, SOLWAY CC, 57 Robb Place, Castle Douglas, Kirkcudbrightshire DG7 1LW

M.J. Hall, SOMERSET & WILTSHIRE ROVER OC, Nightingale Farm, Broome, Swindon, Wilts. SN3 1NA

Mr J. Taylor, SOUTHSEA MC LTD, 'Whiteacre', Meonstoke, Hants SO3 1NP

D.J. Paterson, SOUTH OF SCOTLAND CC LTD, 33 Rae Street, Dumfries DG1 1HY

Miss P. Norman, SOUTH MOLTON & DMC, Great Wadham, Knowstone, South Molton, Devon EX36 4RS

Mr G. Edwards, SOUTHERN ROC LTD, 3 Eton Close, Walderslade, Chatham, Kent ME5 9AT

W.B. Schofield, SOUTH SHORE MSC, 94 Curzon Road, St Annes, Lancashire FY8 3SY

R. Harkness, SOUTH BANK MC, 80 Low Leys Road, Bottesford, Scunthorpe, S. Humberside DN17 2SN

A.J. Tearle, SOUTH BUCKS MC LTD, 85 Harlington Road, Hillingdon, Uxbridge, Middx. UB8 3HZ

Mrs J. Milton, SOUTH DERBYSHIRE MC, 30 Bitham Lane, Stretton, Burton-on-Trent, Staffs.

D. Bates, SOUTH EAST ESSEX AC, 8 Feering Row, Basildon, Essex SS14 1TE

R. Endean, SOUTH HAMS MC LTD, 14 Lansdowne Park, Totnes, Devon

Ms C.E. Grinstead, SOUTHERN CC, Baileys, Antlands Lane East, Shipley Bridge, Nr Horley, Surrey RH6 9TE

I. Howells, SOUTH WALES AC, 33 Gethin Terrace, Porth Rhondda, Mid-Glamorgan CF39 9TT

S. Price, SOUTHERN COUNTIES OFFROADERS, 26 Nuthatch Close, Creekmoor Poole, Dorset BH17 7XR

E.J. Gear, SOUTHERN MILESTONE MC LTD, Wraxhill Farmhouse, Lower Turners Barn Lane, Yeovil, Somerset

P. Dale, SOUTHAMPTON MC, Lower Farm Cottage, Sugar Lane, Longparish, Nr Andover, Hants.

Mr S. Sladdin, SPADEADAM MOTORCLUB, 11 Faustin Hill, Wetheral, Cumbria CA4 8JZ

Mrs D. Parsons, SPORTING OWNERS DC, Tumbleweed, Hillersdon Chase, Stoke Hammond, Milton Keynes

Ms V. Adaway, SPORTS RDC, 70 Nest Lane, Wellingborough, Northants. NN8 4AX

John James Keatley, SPORTING TRIALS CC, 19 Tobermore Road, Magherafelt, Co. Londonderry BT45 5HB

Mr Keith Roberts, SPORTING CC OF NORFOLK, 18 Woodside Park, Attleboroughtead, Norfolk

Mr G. Gaskill, SPRINGHILL MSC, 83 Dill Hall Lane, Church Accrington, Lancashire BB5 4DT

A.E. Alexander, STAFFS AND SHROPSHIRE LRC LTD, 122 Hastings Road, Swadlincote, Burton on Trent DE11 9AJ

S.M. Perren, STAFFORD & DCC, Conifers, Cross Butts, Eccleshall, Staffs. ST21 6AX

K. Daw, ST. HELENS MC, 17 Driffield Road, Prescot, Merseyside L34 1LH

R.D. Milloy, STOCKPORT MC LTD, 21 Larchwood Drive, Wilmslow, Cheshire SK9 2NU

J. Stewart, STOCKTON & DMC LTD, 21 Selwyn Drive, Bishopsgarth, Stockton on Tees TS19 8XF

Allan Paul, STONEHAVEN & DMC, 8 Fittick Place, Cove Bay, Aberdeen AB1 4PJ

Mr M. Ellen, STORT VALLEY AC LTD, 32 Claypit Piece, Saffron Walden, Essex CB11 4DR

N. MacGregor, STRATHCLYDE POLICE MC, Ben View, Gartocharn by Alexandria, Dumbartonshire

H. McGhie, STRANRAER AND DCC, The Elms, Kirkcolm, Stranraer, Scotland DG9 0NT

Mrs M. Dyas, STREETLY MC LTD, 36 Spring Road, Lichfield, Staffordshire WS13 6BJ

N. Moss, STROUD DMC, 99 Bisley Road, Stroud, Gloucestershire

S. Barrell, SUFFOLK FOUR WHEEL DC, 19 Chestnut Close, Stowupland, Stowmarket IP14 4DN

R.D. Baxter, SUNBAC, 5 Hillmorton Road, Knowle, Solihull B93 9JL

P. Shimmell, SUNBEAM TALBOT ALPINE REG, 183 Needlers End Lane, Balsall Common, West Midlands

D.J.H. Parrott, SUNBEAM RAPIER OC, 27 Freshfield Gardens, Waterlooville, Hampshire PO7 7TL

M. Brabrook-Norman, SURREY SPORTING MC, 40 Burgh Wood, Banstead, Surrey SM7 1EP

C. Speare, SUSSEX CC, 2 Westmeston Avenue, Rottingdean, Brighton, East Sussex

Mr P. Stenning, SUTTON & CHEAM MC, 124 Ladygrove, Pixton Way, Forestdale, Croydon, Surrey CR0 9LT

Mrs. A. Whatley, SWINDON PHOENIX CC LTD, 18 Marshfield Way, Stratton St Margaret, Swindon, Wilts. SN3 4PS

M.G. Crocker, SWLMC, Friston, Potmans Lane, Lunsford Cross, Bexhill on Sea, Sussex

D. Dobson, TAUNTON MC LTD, 6 Stoneleigh Court, Pembroke Close, Galmington, Taunton TA1 4LY

B. Thomas, TAVERN MC LTD, c/o Towns Talk Motel, Bridgewater Road, Bristol

Mike Perkin, TAVISTOCK AND DISTRICT LTD, 35 Sycamore Avenue, Bishopsmead, Tavistock, Devon PL19 9NL

K. Elders, TC76 AC OF DARLINGTON, 40 Willow Road, Darlington, Co. Durham DL3 6QA

Teac, The Secretary, THAMES ESTUARY AC, 111 Eastern Esplanade, Southend on Sea, Essex

A. Morris, TELFORD AC LTD, 52 Dunval Road, Bridgnorth, Salop WV16 4NB

J. Worger, THAME MC LTD, 15 Drayton Road, Aylesbury, Buckinghamshire HP20 2EN

D.A. James, THAMES VALLEY MC, 11 Rowley Close, Wembley, Middlesex HA0 4HE

William Heaney, THOROUGHBRED SPORTS CC NI, 39 Ashley Drive, Bangor, Co. Down BT20 5RD

Mr R. Fellows, TORBAY MOTOR CLUB LTD, 30 York Road, Paignton, Devon TQ4 5NW

B. Dove, TRACKROD MC LTD, 5 Kenilworth Gardens, Gildersome, Leeds LS27 7EW

H. Davies, TRIUMPH SPORTS SIX CLUB LTD, 21 Friars Croft, Calmore, Totton, Hants SO4 2SS

D.R. Kavanagh, TRIUMPH SPORTING OC, 5 Burleigh Close, Hazel Grove, Cheshire SK7 5QT

Mr I. Cook, TRIUMPH SPORTS C C-BRISTOL, 19 Somerset Road, Portishead, Bristol BS20 8EE

Alan Williams, TRIUMPH TR CAR CLUB, 2 Bryn Hyfryd, Coedpoeth, Wrexham, Clwyd LL11 3YA

Mrs A. Williams, TROSTRE MC, 25 Station Road, Grovesend, Swansea, S Wales SA4 2GY

Mrs V. Simpson, TR REGISTER, 271 High Street, Berkhamsted, Herts. HP4 1AA

R.P. Duckworth, TRURO AND DMC, Glenesk, Tolgus Mount, Redruth, Cornwall TR15 3SU

D. Welch, TUNBRIDGE WELLS MC LTD, 67 Whetsted Road, Five Oak Green, Nr Tonbridge, Kent TN12 6RT

M. Shaw, TVR CC, 74 Holmuood Road, Seven Kings, Ilford, Essex IG3 9XZ

Mrs J. Collinson, TWO COUNTIES KART CLUB, 33 Petwyn Close, Tricketts Cross, Ferndown, Dorset BH22 8BG

R. Wilkinson, 2300 CLUB, 12 Shetland Close, Wilpshire, Blackburn, Lancs. BB1 9NQ

J.T. Telford, TYNEMOUTH & DMSC LTD, The Clubhouse, Billy Mill Lane, North Shields, Tyne and Wear

Mrs S Cairns, ULSTER KC LTD, 5 Thornleigh Close, Lisburn, Co. Antrim, N. Ireland BT28 2DB

Mr R. Daniel, ULSTER VINTAGE CC, 1 Roslyn Avenue, Bangor, Co. Down, Northern Ireland BT20 4WW

I. Busby, ULSTER UNIV MC, 55 Sandhill Gardens, Knock, Belfast BT5 6FF

Mrs C. Kernahan, ULSTER AC LTD, 3 Botanic Avenue, Belfast BT17 1JG, Northern Ireland

J.C. Gilbert, UTD HOSP. & UNIV. LONDON MC, 1 Pear Tree Dell, Letchworth, Herts. SG6 2SW

Mark Kent, UNIV. HOSP. OF WALES MC, 3 Parkfield Place, Maindy, Cardiff

Miss J. Cross, UNIVERSITY OF BRADFORD MC, Sports Centre, Univ. of Bradford, Richmond Road, Bradford

M.A. Chadwick, UNIVERSITY OF LIVERPOOL MC, 1 Drayton Close, Irby, Wirral, Merseyside

Mrs M. Milroy, UPPER NITHSDALE CC, 45 Craigens Road, Craigens, Cumnock, Ayrshire KA18 3AX

Mrs H.M. Beechinor, VAGABOND MC, 26 Hollis Street, Alvaston, Derby DE2 8QU

K. Morgan, VALE OF COTHI MC, 38 Newtown, Penybanc, Ammanford, Dyfed SA18 3RS

I. Turner, VAUXHALL MOTORING SECTION, 38 Aintree Close, Bletchley, Bucks.

A.P. Kay, VAUXHALL MOTORING GROUP (W), 151 Singleton Avenue, Prenton, Birkenhead, Merseyside L42 9JW

Mrs J. Innes-Ker, VETERAN CC OF GB, Jessamine House, High Street, Ashwell, Nr Baldock, Herts. SF7 5NL

L. Bell, VICKERS BARROW MC, 8 Brighton Street, Barrow in Furness, Cumbria

E.B.E Smith, VINTAGE SPORTS CC, 121 Russell Road, Newbury, Berks. RG14 5JX

S.G. Mills, VOLKSWAGEN OC GB, 4 Bredon Avenue, Birchen Coppice, Kidderminster DY11 7EP

Mrs C. Boothroyd, WAKEFIELD & DMSC, 3 Woodend Avenue, Cubley, Penistone, Sheffield S30 6FX

J.R.A. Hunt, WALLASEY MC LTD, 102A Seaview Road, Wallasey, Merseyside L45 4LD

J.K. Rudd, WARRINGTON & DMC, 9 Montclare Crescent, Stockton Heath, Warrington, Cheshire

Mr P.K. Hurst, WELSH COUNTIES CC, 48 Newzealand Road, Cathays, Cardiff CF4 3BS

Mrs C. Morris, WELSH BORDER CC LTD, 1 Llys Avenue, Oswestry, Shropshire SY11 2XE

Mr S. Barnard, WESSEX MC, Students Union, Southampton Univ., Highfield, Southampton SO9 5NH

R. Miller, WEST OF SCOTLAND KC, 57G Chapel Street, Airdrie, Scotland

C. Rees, WEST ESSEX CC LTD, 401/403 Rayleigh Road, Benfleet, Essex SS7 3ST

H. Luke-Dunne, WEST CORNWALL MC LTD, The Premier Garage, Causeway Head, Penzance, Cornwall TR18 2ST

G. Powell, WEST SUFFOLK MC LTD, 37 Kings Road, Glemsford, Sudbury, Suffolk

Mrs L. Givens, WESTON SUPER MARE MC, 4 Langleys Cottages, Clapton, Nr Bath

B.G. Whittaker, WESTMORLAND MC LTD, 11 Long Meadow Lane, Natland, Nr Kendal, Cumbria LA9 7QZ

D.R. Stanforth, WEST LANCASHIRE MC, 93 Sefton Street, Southport, Merseyside PR8 5DD

Miss C. McMullen, WEST CUMBERLAND MC, 25 Duke Street, Cleator Moor, Whitehaven, Cumbria

Paul Price, WEST MIDLANDS POLICE MC, 10 Leahouse Road, Oldbury, Warley, West Midlands B68 8PD

A. Jose, WHICKHAM & DMC LTD, 10 St Georges Terrace, Bells Close, Lemington, Newcastle upon Tyne NE15 6YA

R.P. Dewey, WHITE HORSE MC, 85 Abbots Wood, Yate, Bristol BS17 4NF

Mr C. Dobson, WHITBY & DMC, 29 Marshall Drive, Brotton Saltburn, Cleveland TS12 2RD

K. Ikin, WHITCHURCH MC, 2 Park Road, Whitchurch, Shropshire SY13 1HR

D. Cornwall, WICKFORD AC, 25 Belmont Avenue, Wickford, Essex SS12 0HP

D. Hind, WIGAN & DMC, 3 Norfolk Road, Longshaw Billinge, Nr Wigan, Lancs. WN5 7JR

G.T. Forrester, WIGTON MC LTD, 1 Springfields, Wigton, Cumbria CA7 9JT

R.J. Copeland, WINCHESTER AND DCC, 53 Cambrian Way, Basingstoke, Hants. RG22 5AH

I. Bartlett, WINDSOR CC LTD, 6 Crosswell Close, Charlton Rd, Shepperton, Middx. TW17 0ST

Ms S. White, WITHAM & DMC, 75 Victoria Street, Braintree, Essex CM7 6HL

S. Bradley, WITNEY MC, 104 Farmers Close, Witney, Oxon OX8 6NR

Mrs A Wright, WOMBWELL SYKC, 19 Clarksfield Street, Oldham, Lancs. OL4 3AW

J.M. Bounden, WOLSELEY HORNET SPECIAL C, Rookery Barn, Sandpit Lane, Bledlow, Aylesbury, Bucks. HP17 9QQ

D.E. Allen, WOLSELEY REGISTER, Glenville, Glynde Road, Bexley Heath, Kent DA7 4EU

Mrs J.E. Arnold, WOLVES & SOUTH STAFFS CC, 97 Greyhound Lane, Norton, Stourbridge, West Midlands

M.R. Briant, WOOLBRIDGE MC, 2 Lindens Close, Weymouth, Dorset DT4 7LN

Mr Peter Monkhouse, WORKINGTON DMC, 4 Asby Road, Asby, Workington, Cumbria

Mrs C.A. Lockwood, WORKSOP AND DMC, 130 Station Road, Kiveton Park, Sheffield S31 8QQ

Dave Barrell, WYE & WELSH ROVER OWNERS, 22 Prince's Walk, New Inn, Pontypool, Gwent

Miss M. Johns, YEOVIL CC LTD, 148 Monks Dale, Yeovil, Somerset

Miss L. Hartley, YORK MC LTD, 70 Main Street, Knapton, York

Mrs S. Whiteley, YORKSHIRE ROC LTD, 10 Thorncliffe, Kirkburton, Huddersfield, West Yorkshire HD8 0UG

Mr T. Bilham, YORKSHIRE SCC LTD, 11 Broadlands, Shann Park, Keighley BD20 6HX

B. Walton, YORKSHIRE BANK MC, Holly Tree Cottage, Dairy Lane, Darley, Harrogate, N Yorks HG3 2QW

A. Cook, YSTRAD MYNACH MOTOR CLUB, 5 Oxwich Close, Carn Gethin Farm Est, Hengoed, Mid Glam, CF8 7JB

Nicholas Spearman, THE 061 MOTOR CLUB, 56 Glandon Drive, Cheadle Hume, Stockport, Cheshire SK8 7EY

M. Bolgerng, NAT WEST BANK MC (THAMES), 241 Peach Road, Queens Park, London W10 4DX

R.S. Davis, BARCLAYS BANK MIDLANDS, 477 Warwick Road, Solihull, West Midlands B91 1AN

Mrs L.F. Neal, ASSO. OF CENTRAL SOUTHERN MC, 60 Hillsboro Road, Bognor Regis, West Sussex PO21 2DY

D. James, ASSO. OF EASTERN MC, 11 Rowley Close, Wembley, Middlesex HA0 4HE

John Pickup, EAST MIDS ASSO. OF MC, 298 Tythbarn Lane, Tidbury Green, Solihull B90 1PHL

I. Lawrie, EAST OF SCOTLAND ASSO. OF CC, 27 Clermiston Road, Edinburgh EH12 6XD

A. Biss, LONDON COUNTIES ASSO. OF MC, 6 Wavertree Road, South Woodford, London E18 1BL

M. Lucas, ASSO. OF MIDLANDS MC, 29 Avondale Close, Kingswinford, Dudley DY6 7HJ

K.W. Kirtley, ASSO. OF N.E. & CUMBRIA CC, 121 Lamonby Close, Nunthorpe, Middlesbrough TS7 0QG

J.B. Wilkinson, ASSO. OF N.E. MIDLANDS MC, 1 Bayons Avenue, Springfield, Grimsby DN33 3LN

J.H. Richardson, ASSO. OF NORTHERN CC, 67 West Park, Selby, North Yorkshire YO8 0JN

N. Moffitt, ASSO. OF N. IRELAND CC, 34 Jersey Avenue, Lisburn, Co. Antrim BT27 4BJ

A. Dean-Lewis, ASSO. OF NORTH WESTERN CC, 44 Penryn Isaf Road, Penrhyn Bay, Colwyn Bay, Clwyd LL30 3LT

Ms M. Greeland, ASSO. OF SOUTH EASTERN MC, 8 Great Queen Street, Dartford, Kent DA1 1TJ

R.B. Mayo, ASSO. OF SOUTH WESTERN MC, 88 Queensholm Drive, Downend, Bristol

F.K. Williams, WELSH ASSO. OF MC, Haulfan, Llanbedr DC, Nr Ruthin LL15 1UT

J. Arnold, ASSO. OF WEST MIDLAND MC, Wharf Cottage, Longdon on Tern, Shropshire TF6 6LQ

D. Attwood, ASSO. OF W. OF SCOTLAND MSC, Jura, Larg Road, Stranraer, Wigtownshire DG9 0JE

APPENDIX 2:
GLOSSARY

CART America's leading single-seater racing series. Cars often known as Indycars in deference to the most prestigious race in the annual calendar, the Indianapolis 500.

CLUBMANS Open two-seater sports car formula, running in two classes. The first allows for modified 1.6 litre or modified 1.7 litre engines, the second for motors to FF1600 specification.

FORMULA 1 Cars competing in official World Championship Grands Prix, as sanctioned by the sport's governing body, the FISA. Single-seater chassis powered by 3.5 litre normally-aspirated engines. Turbochargers banned from 1989.

FORMULA 2 Formerly the final stepping stone for a driver aspiring to F1. Phased out of Europe at the end of 1984, and killed off in Japan two years later. Now defunct, replaced by Formula 3000.

FORMULA 3 Single-seaters with 2 litre engines, power of which is regulated by an air inlet restrictor. Basis for main national racing championships in Britain, France, Germany, Italy and Sweden.

FORMULA 4 Single-seater formula for cars running either tuned Chrysler 1 litre or less modified pushrod Ford 1.3 litre engines.

FORMULA 750 Two-seater sports car formula, using Reliant engines up to 857 cc.

FORMULA 1300 Two-seater sports car formula, using 1.3 litre pushrod engines.

FORMULA 3000 Three-litre single-seater formula brought in to replace F2 in 1985. Now recognized as best breeding ground for potential Grand Prix stars. Engines governed by rev limiter, which improves reliability and longevity and thus keeps costs down.

FORMULA ATLANTIC/PACIFIC Highly-tuned 1.6 litre engines in chassis nearer to F3000 specifications than to F3. Once popular in UK. Now defunct here, although thriving in America and the Antipodes.

FORMULA FIRST Launched in 1987 to reintroduce cheaper single-seater racing for the aspiring youngster. Concept similar to Formula Ford, but without such scope for development (to keep costs down). Power from 1.6 litre Ford CVH engines.

FORMULA FORD 1600   Initiative of Brands Hatch MD John Webb back in 1967. Now the most popular single-seater racing formula anywhere in the world. Cars powered by 1.6 litre Ford engines, running on treaded tyres.

FORMULA FORD 2000   Descended from FF1600. Power comes from 2 litre Ford units, and cars run racing tyres and aerodynamic wings.

FORMULA FORWARD   New single seater category in 1989, designed to appeal to graduates from Formula First and Formula Ford. All chassis and engines identical.

FORMULA SUPER VEE   Defunct in Europe, but alive and well in the USA. Race-tuned 1.6 litre VW engines provide performance on a par with F3.

FORMULA VAUXHALL/OPEL LOTUS   Introduced in 1988 as new training formula for young drivers. Single-seaters powered by 2 litre engine direct off the Opel production line in Russelsheim.

FORMULA VEE   Popular with amateurs. Low-cost single-seater racing, based around engine and suspension components from 1.3 litre VW Beetle.

GROUP A   Internationally recognized saloon car formula. World Rally Championship and European Touring Car Championship run to Group A regulations, along with many of the world's major rally and saloon series.

GROUP B   Formerly basis of the World Rally Championship. Cars loosely-based around production models, but highly modified to give staggering performance capabilities. Spate of accidents persuaded the FISA to outlaw them from further rally competition, although some cars went on to be used in rallycross.

GROUP C/C2   Two-seater sports car formula, basis for World Sports-Prototype Championship. Cars are governed by weight limits, and by their ability to cover a given distance on an accepted fuel allocation. C2 cars get less fuel allowance, and are slightly slower than their counterparts.

GROUP N   Saloon car formula allowing very few modifications to standard production car.

IMSA   America's equivalent of Group C, similar cars running to slightly different regulations.

MODIFIED SALOONS Tuned saloon cars which must retain the silhouette of the original model. Engine block and cylinder head must be identifiable as that of the original model.
MONOPOSTO Single-seater formula from which professionals are barred. Several engine options available, all providing similar performance. There is also a Monoposto Kent class, allowing lightly modified FF1600 engines, racing slicks and wings.
MULTISPORTS Introduced in 1989 as a relatively low-cost sports car Formula featuring identical chassis.
NASCAR Known in the USA as stock cars. British stock cars race on oval circuits at speeds of up to 60 mph. These large, powerful saloons will lap America's banked circuits at over 200mph …
PRODUCTION SALOONS Formula unique to Britain. Saloon cars running strictly limited modifications.
SPECIAL SALOONS Tuned saloon car formula. Engine must be located as that on original car, but need not necessarily be of same manufacture. Certain aerodynamic aids also permitted.
SPORTS 2000 Category for two-seater, open-top racing cars running to FF2000 engine regulations.